THIRD BOOK OF WOODEN TOYS

W. G. Alton

Principal Lecturer, Trent Park
College of Education

MILLS & BOON LIMITED, LONDON

By the same author:
METAL PROJECTS—FURNITURE
MORE WOODWORK PROJECTS
WOODEN TOYS THAT YOU CAN MAKE
MORE WOODEN TOYS THAT YOU CAN MAKE

First published in Great Britain 1974
by Mills & Boon Limited, 17–19 Foley Street,
London W1A 1DR
Copyright © W. G. Alton 1974
ISBN 0 263 05590 6

Filmset and printed in Great Britain by
Thomson Litho Ltd., East Kilbride

Contents

Preface

This third book of toys to make in wood illustrates that this is a wide field of creativity, giving satisfaction to the maker and giver of a toy as well as to the child who plays with it. The designs I give presuppose that the reader already has experience of some of the basic skills of woodworking, and will want to work out his own ideas for himself. So my instructions are not detailed; but they pass on certain techniques and know-how acquired after much trial and error. I hope this guidance will be helpful and stimulating.

Suggestions for finishing the wood by means of paints and varnishes are given at the back of the book, together with suggestions for making a sawing block and drilling jig.

Metric measurements given in this book are alternative measurements and are not exact equivalents.

W.G.A.

Sand Rake and Hoe

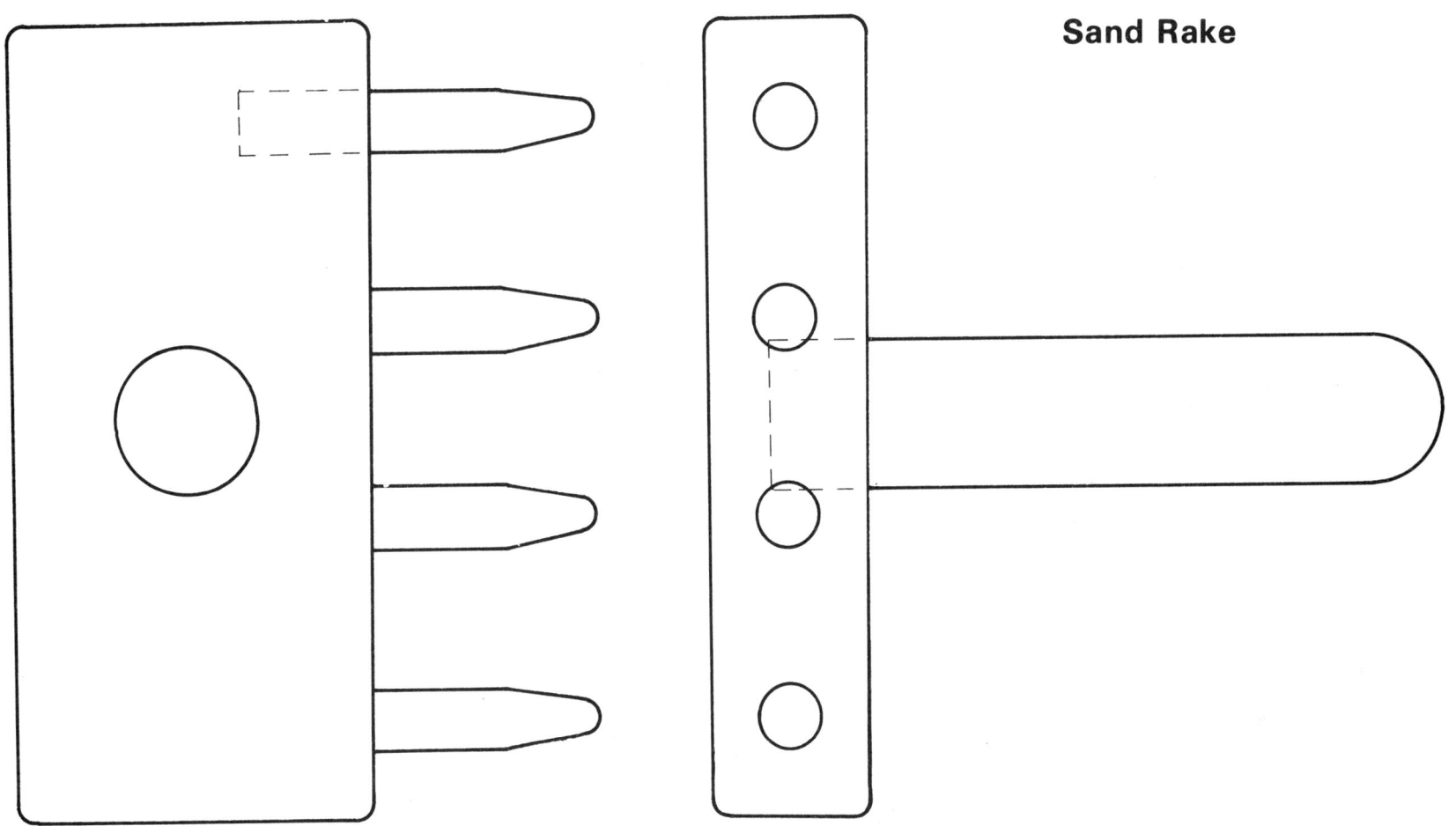

Sand Rake

This attractive toy is easy to use. It is made from beech and finished with a clear lacquer, although it could be painted (see page 96). The handle is made from a piece of broom handle, and the end can be turned or shaped by hand. The points are made from $\frac{3}{8}''$ (9mm) dowel and the ends can be turned or shaped by hand, in which case they are easiest to work if left on a length until the shaping is complete. A waterproof glue can be used, or the parts can be held together quite securely with thin nails.

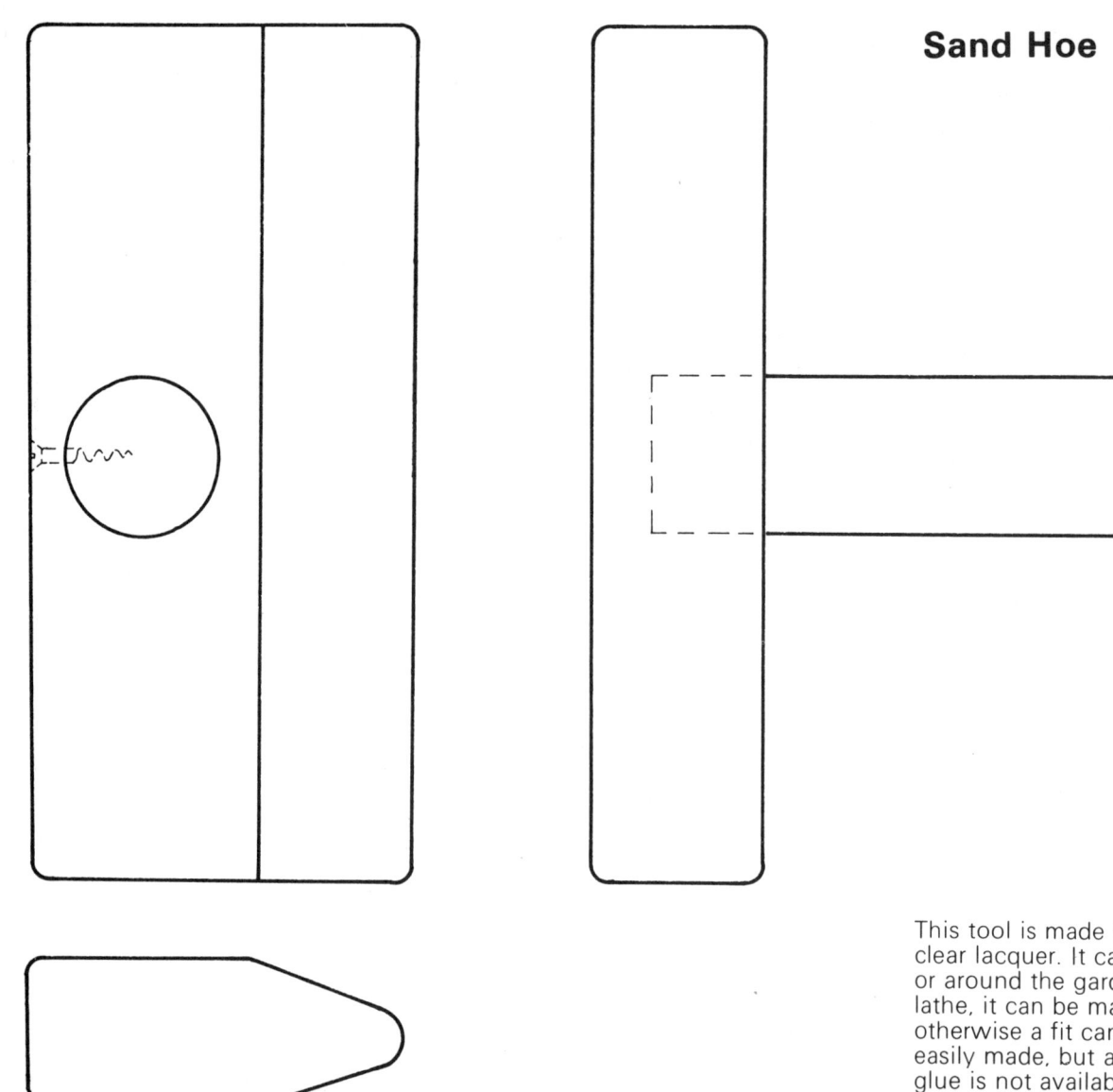

Sand Hoe

This tool is made from beech and is finished with a clear lacquer. It can be used in a sand pit or sand bin, or around the garden. If the handle is turned on a lathe, it can be made to fit precisely into a drilled hole; otherwise a fit can be made with a rasp. A taper fit is easily made, but a parallel fit is less likely to fail. If a glue is not available, a screw or nail can be used to secure the handle. For lacquering, see page 96.

Sand Spade and Rammer

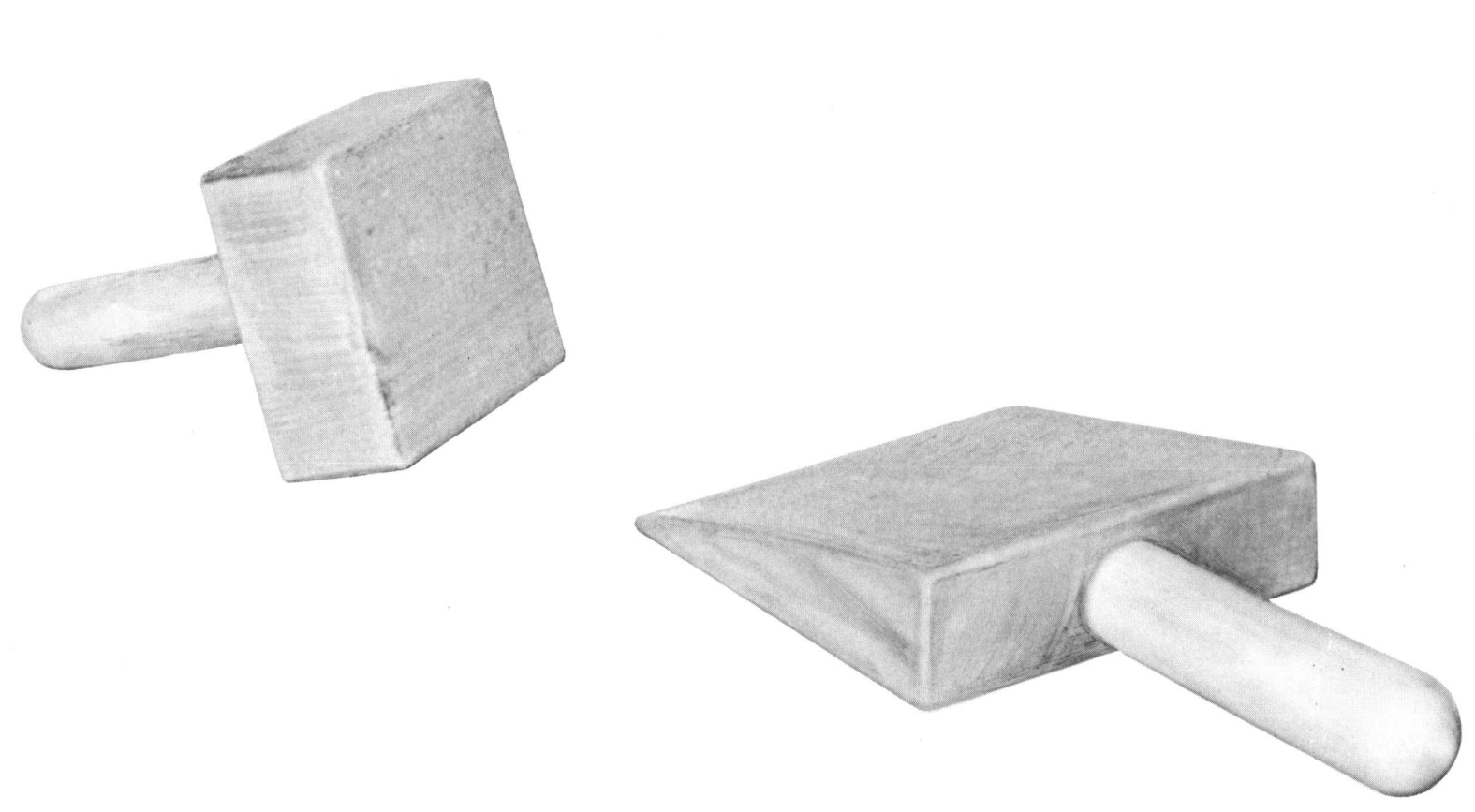

Sand Spade

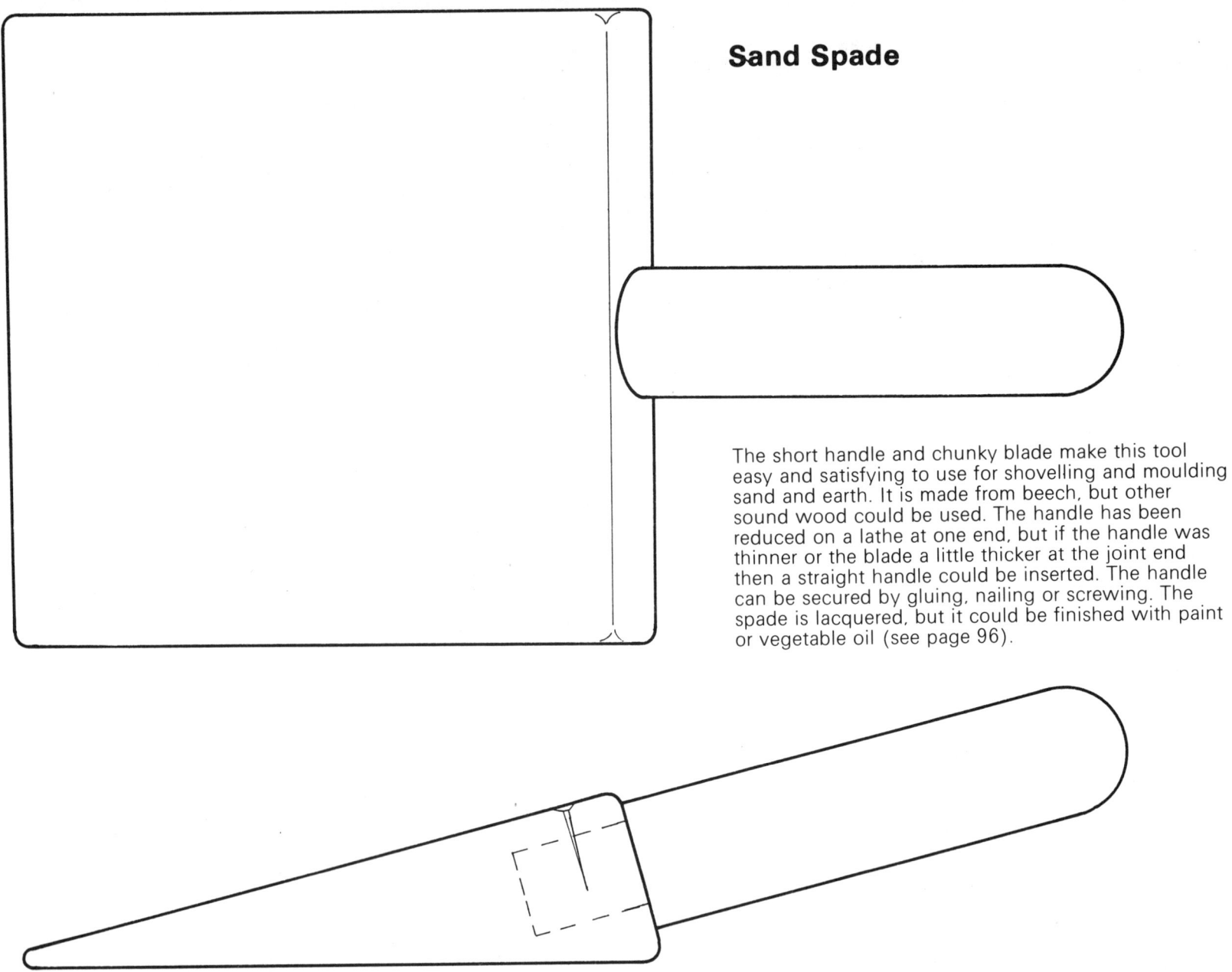

The short handle and chunky blade make this tool easy and satisfying to use for shovelling and moulding sand and earth. It is made from beech, but other sound wood could be used. The handle has been reduced on a lathe at one end, but if the handle was thinner or the blade a little thicker at the joint end then a straight handle could be inserted. The handle can be secured by gluing, nailing or screwing. The spade is lacquered, but it could be finished with paint or vegetable oil (see page 96).

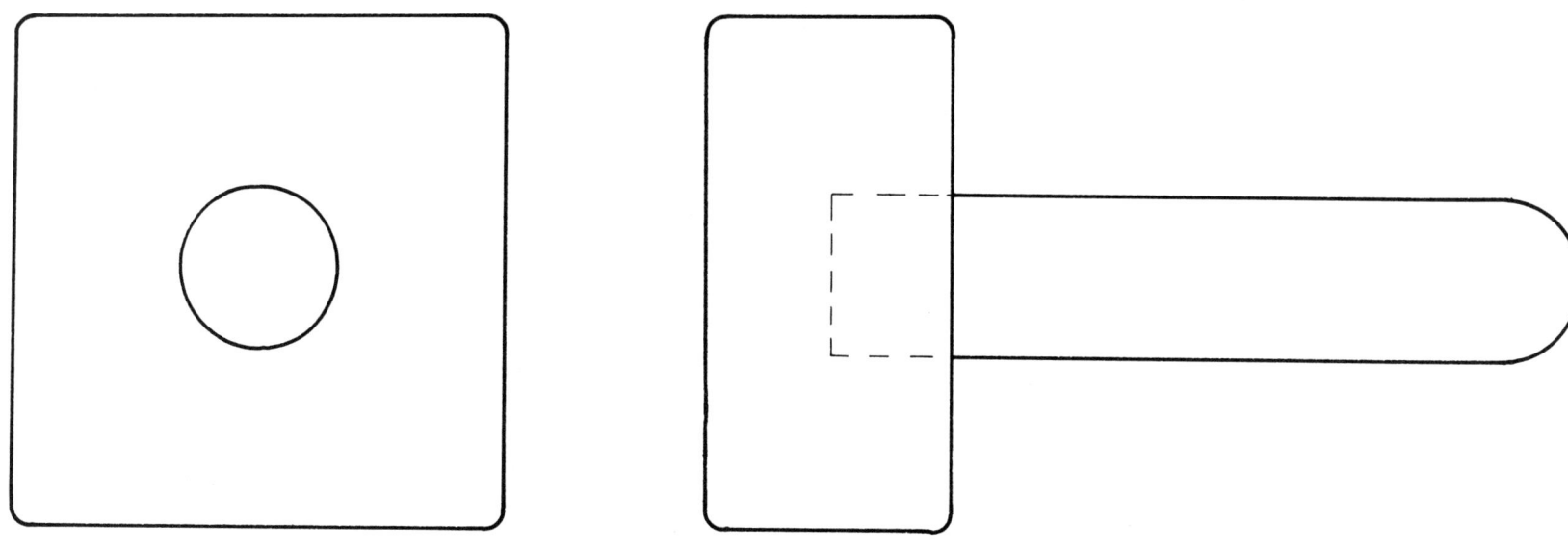

Sand Rammer

This tool is made from beech and lacquered, although
a vegetable oil finish would be quite suitable. Any
other wood could be used, and a nail or screw would
secure the handle. A bright gloss paint would make an
alternative attractive finish. For painting, see page 96.

Small Removal Van

Small Removal Van

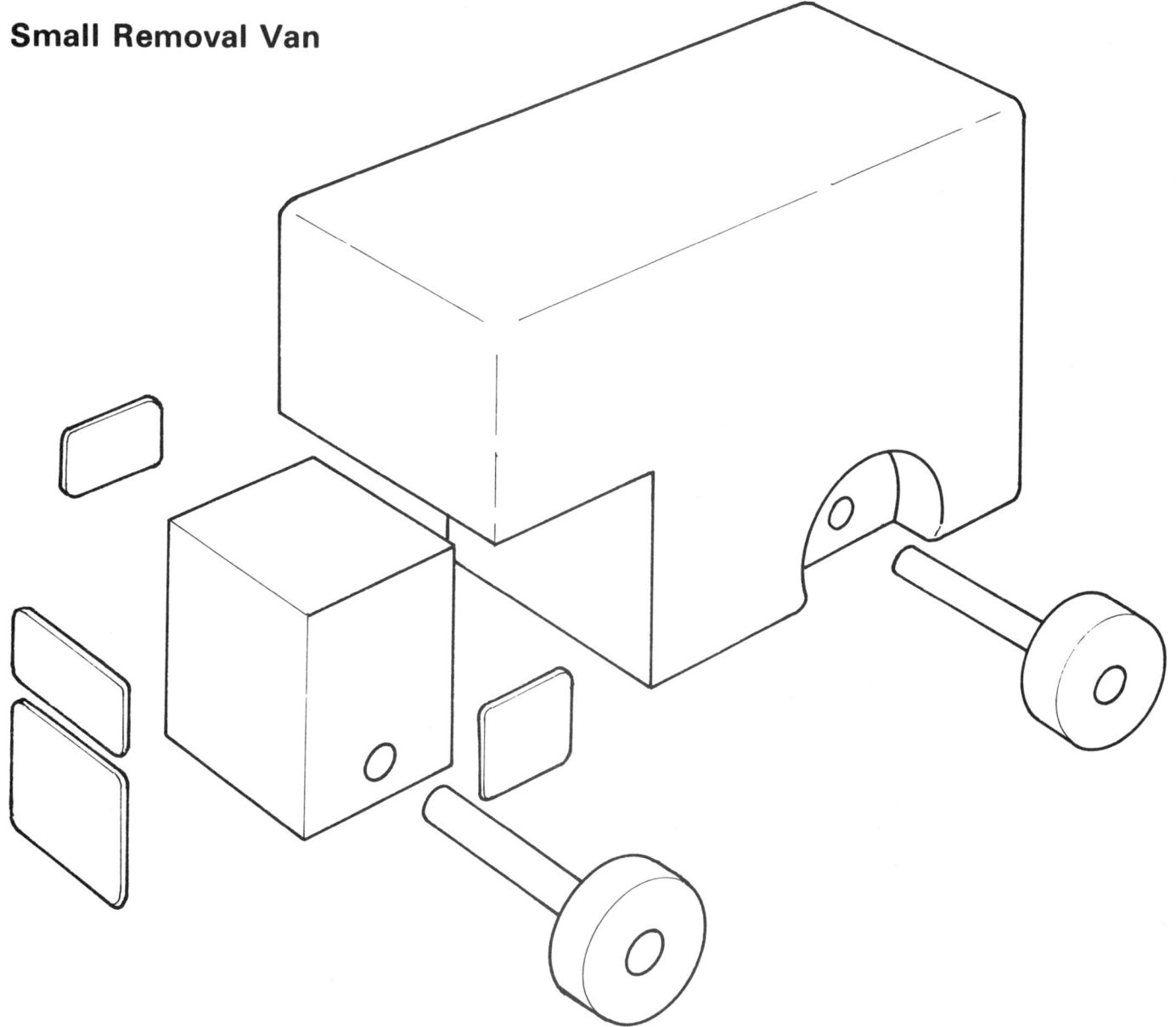

Small Removal Van

This toy is made from a block of wood 6″ × 3¼″ × 2¼″ (150 × 80 × 60mm). The block for the cabin can be sawn and chiselled from the solid or sawn from the block, reduced and glued back into position. The wheels, which are $\frac{7}{16}$″. (10mm) thick, can be cut from large diameter broom handle or turned on a lathe. The axles are cut from $\frac{3}{8}$″ (9mm) dowel and glued into the $\frac{3}{8}$″ wheel holes (page 95). A little candle wax on the axles where they pass through the blocks will allow them to turn freely. The holes in the blocks should be drilled slightly over $\frac{3}{8}$″. Drill the rear wheel housings first, otherwise there will be no centre for the 1½″

(40mm) machine forstner bit. The wheel housings are drilled ½″ (12mm) deep, so that the wheels are level with the outside of the van, apart from the small clearance inside to allow the wheels to turn freely. Plastic panels (not shown in the photograph) can be added to show windows and radiator grill. The windows are cut from white plastic laminate and the radiator grill is also cut from laminate, but of a different colour. The body can be painted or varnished —or the cabin only. The wheels can be painted on the outsides or left as plain wood.

Train

Train

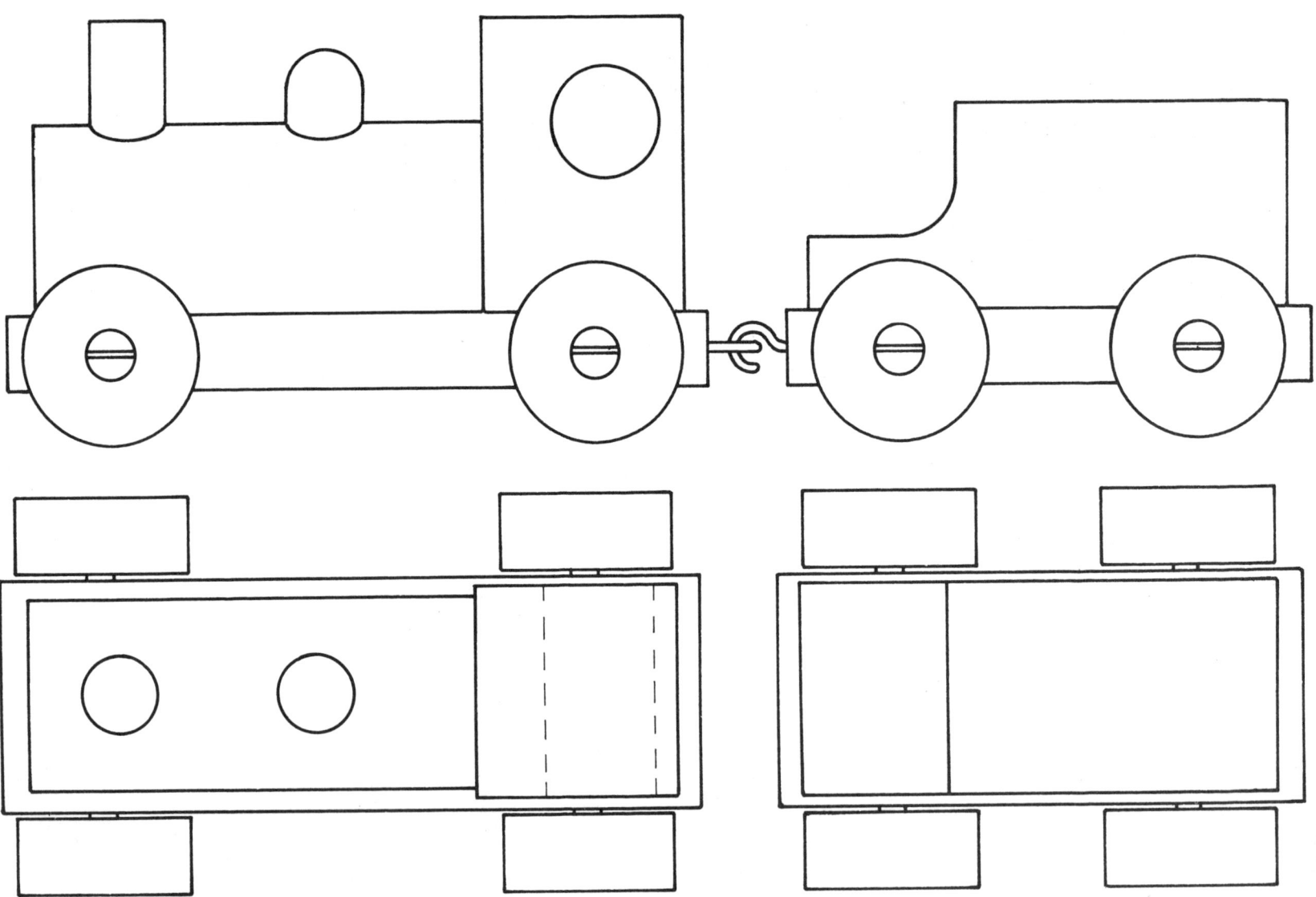

Train

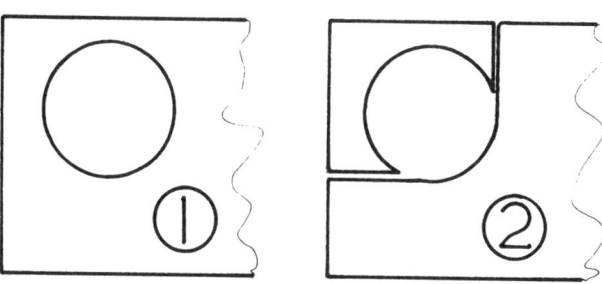

Drilling and shaping the tender

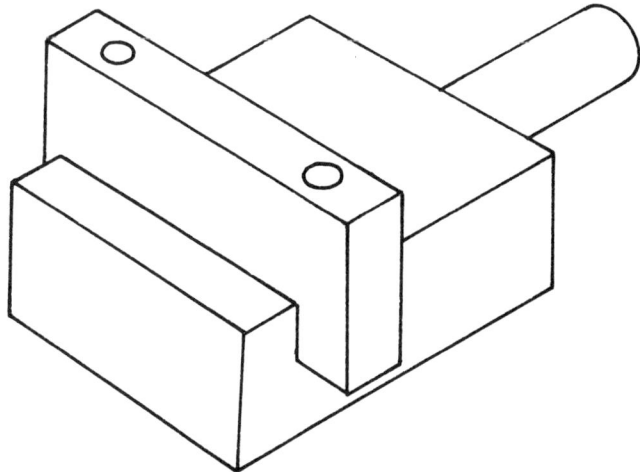

Base block set in machine vice for drilling dowel holes

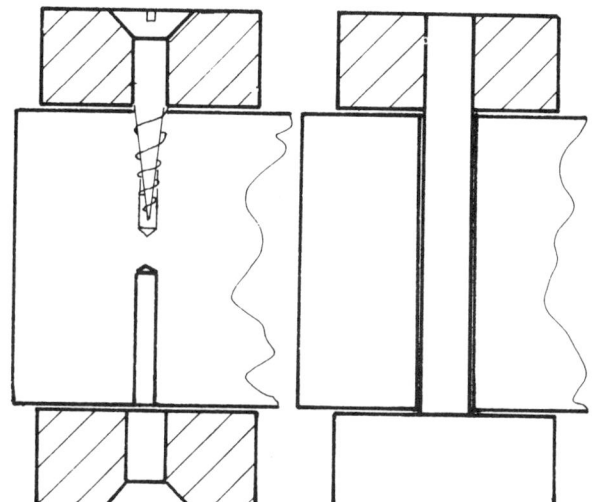

Drilling for screws   Dowel axle

This is an interesting toy to make, and would be a very acceptable gift. The toy shown is made from beech, but any sound wood could be used. The base pieces are made from $1\frac{1}{2}'' \times \frac{5}{8}''$ (38 × 16mm), and the tender and cabin from $1\frac{3}{8}''$ (35mm) square material. The boiler and the wheels were turned in one length and then sawn off (page 94). They could be cut from large diameter broom handle and drilled in the drilling jig (page 95). The wheels are drilled and countersunk for $1'' \times 8$ countersunk screws (round heads would do). $\frac{1}{4}''$ (6mm) dowel could be used for axles, which would pass right through holes $\frac{5}{16}''$ (8mm) in the base blocks. The funnel is cut from $\frac{1}{2}''$ (12mm) dowel. All parts are glued together. A small screw hook and screw eye make ideal connectors.

Cars

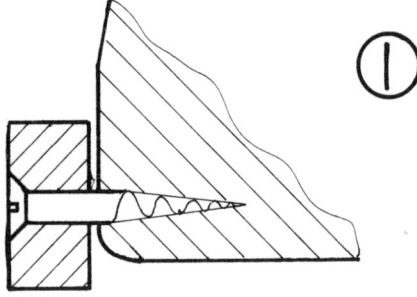

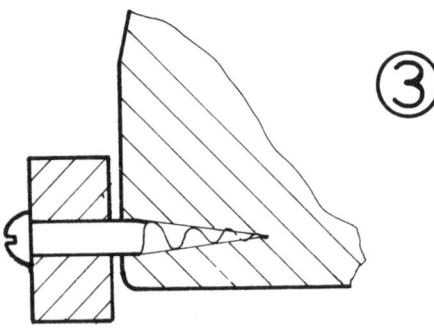

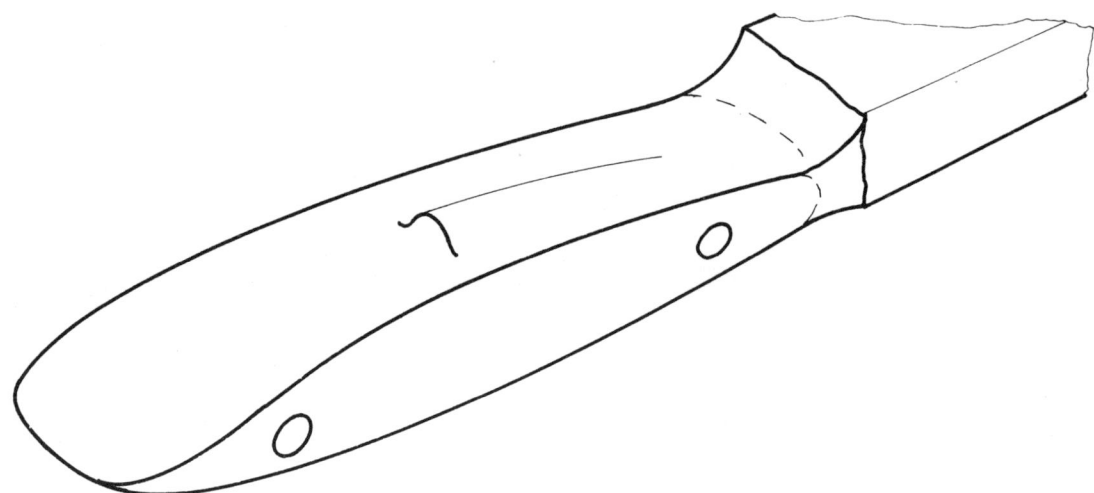

These toys are cut from single pieces of wood which can be kept longer than the toy until most of the tooling, shaping and smoothing is finished (see sketch above). If the side elevation is marked and cut from thin cardboard, then this template can be marked round on both sides, which should be planed clean. The usual tools—tenon saw, coping saw, chisels, cabinet rasps and various grades of glasspaper—can be used. The windows are cut from white plastic laminate and glued on. Alternatively, they could be carefully painted on with a pencil brush, or this feature could be omitted altogether. It is worth remembering that greater squareness of drilling can be achieved if this is done before the block is shaped. For painting see page 96.

1 Countersunk screw used for axle
2 $\frac{1}{4}''$ (6mm) dowel used for axle through an oversize body hole
3 Round-headed screw used for axle.

Cars

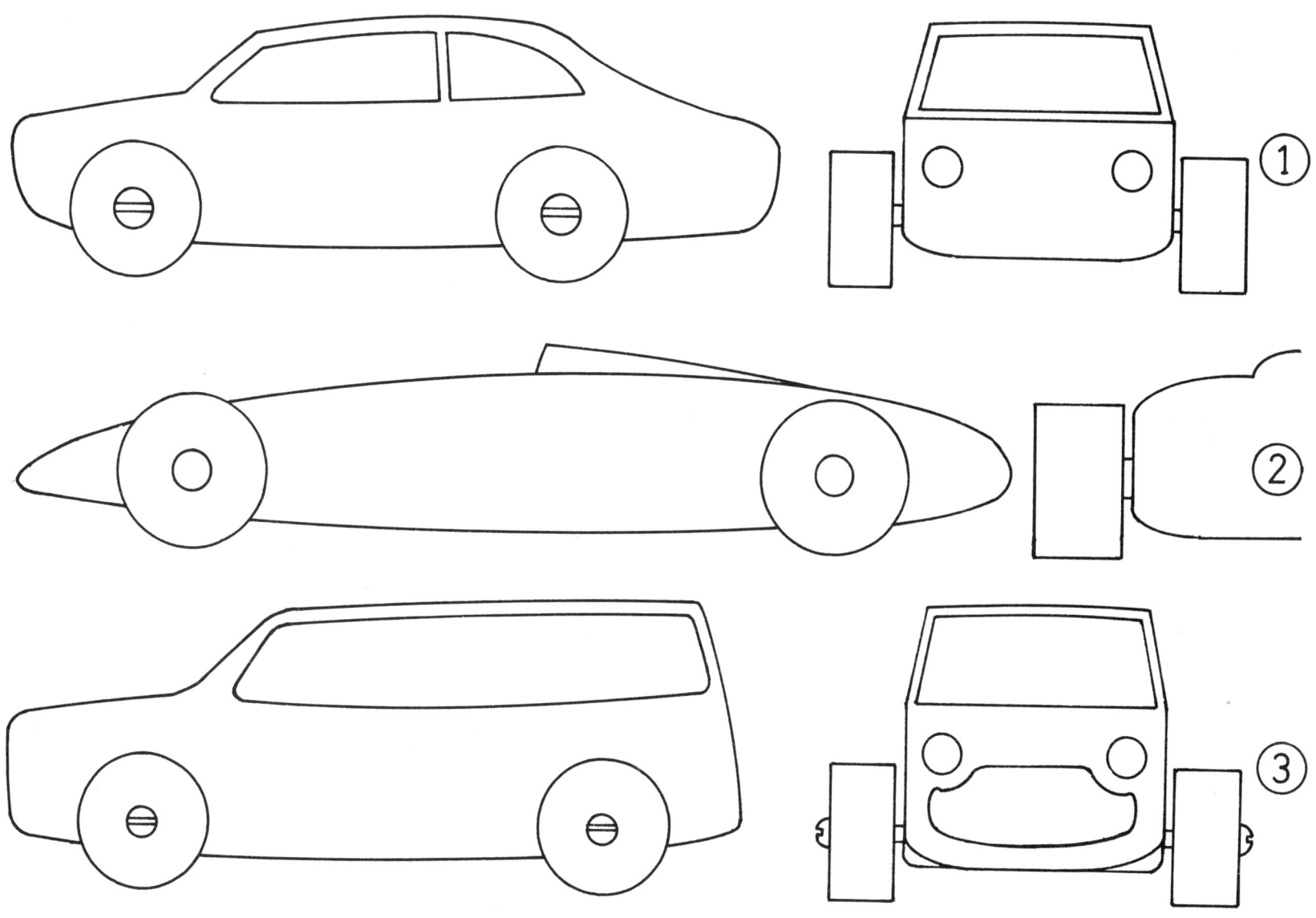

Monkey Acrobat

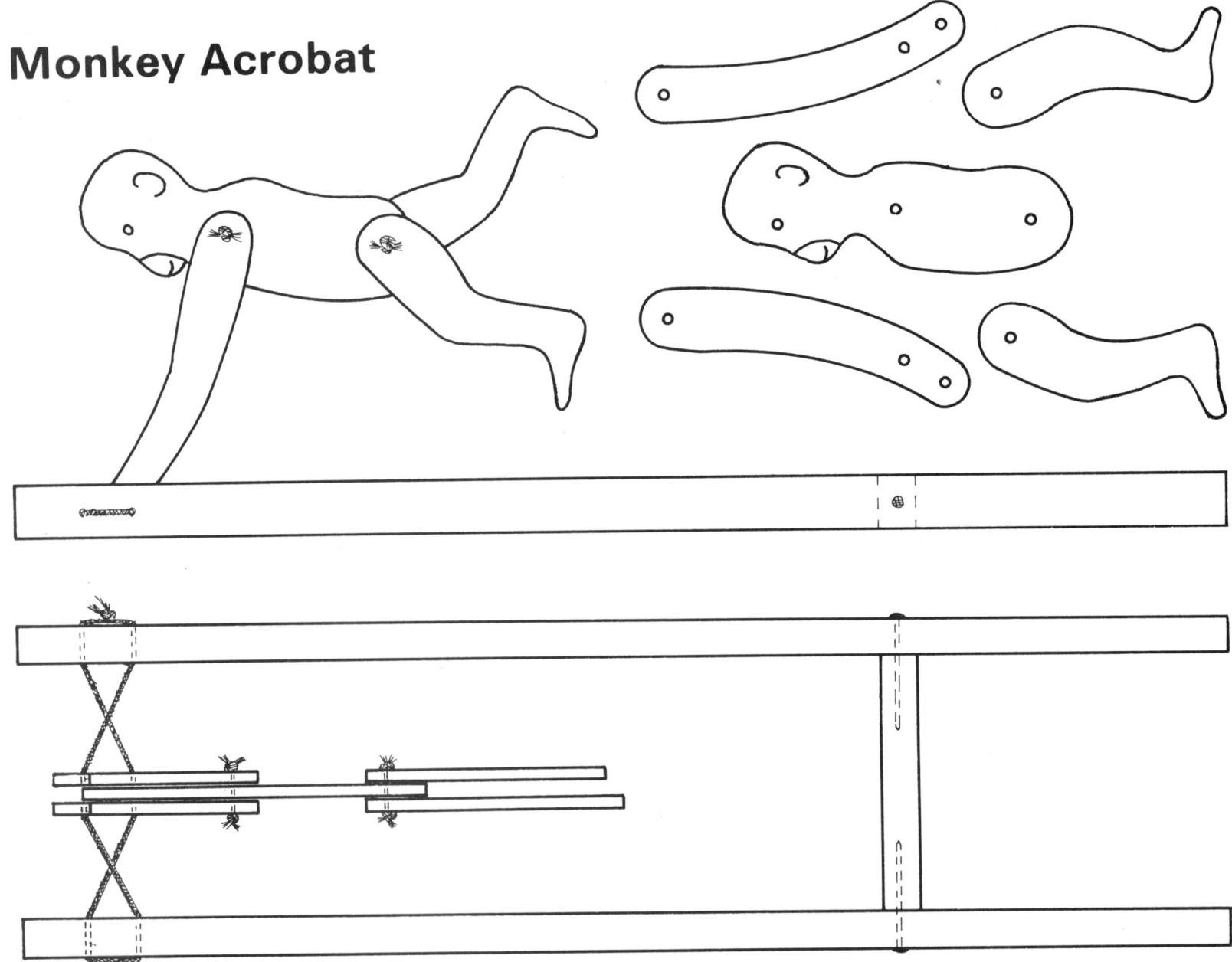

Monkey Acrobat

This is a fascinating little toy—irresistible, quite regardless of how many times it has been played with. There is absolutely no skill required, only a slight pressure and release on the lower sticks; yet it is quite easy to delude oneself into thinking that it is extremely demanding to establish the finer touches. It is a charming way in which to pass a few minutes contemplating the athletic prowess of Anthropopithecus Troglodytes (the Chimpanzee).

The sticks and crossbars are made from $\frac{1}{4}'' \times \frac{3}{8}''$ (6 × 9mm) material. Single, very thin $\frac{3}{8}''$ nails (veneer pins) keep the crossbar in place. The monkey parts are cut out with a piercing saw or a fret-saw from 2 or 3mm ply. They comprise two arms, two legs and a body with head. Holes of $\frac{1}{16}''$ (2mm) diameter are drilled into the body and limbs as shown. The arms and legs are attached loosely to the body with very thin twine. Two holes are drilled at the 'hand' end of the arms, and near the tops of the sticks. The thin twine is passed through these in a single loop when the monkey is held above and upside down (see small sketch). All parts can be painted or stained before assembly, and a monkey face can be painted on the head, if desired.

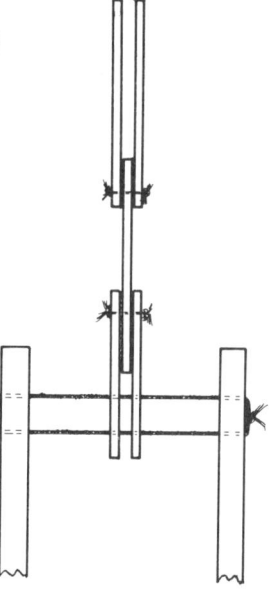

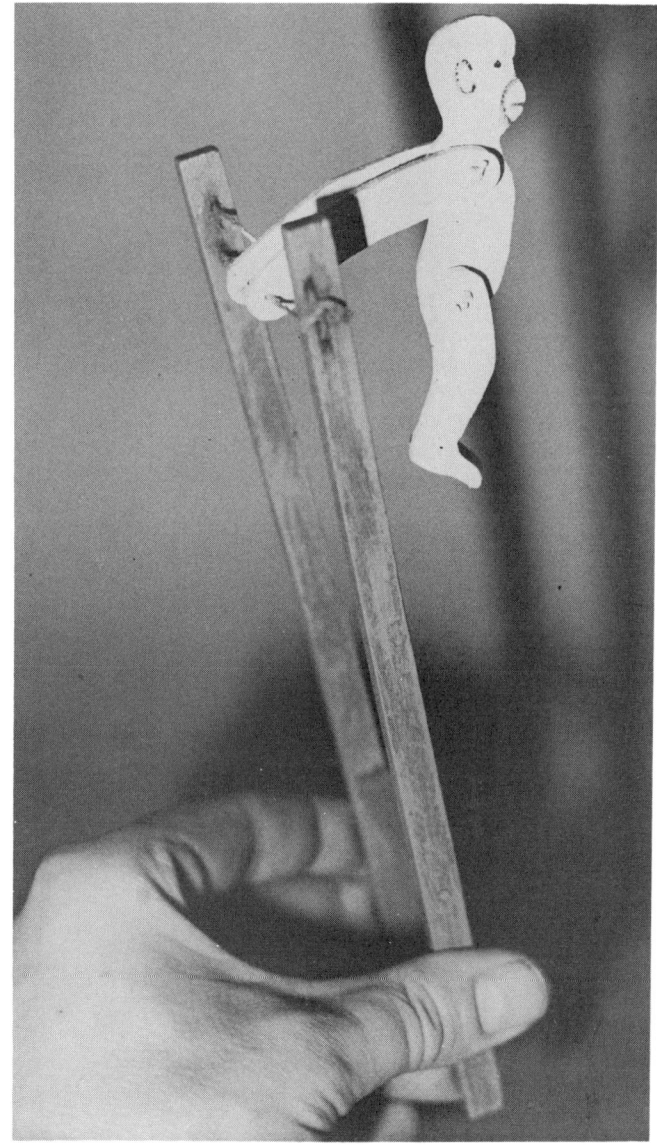

Seesaw

Seesaw

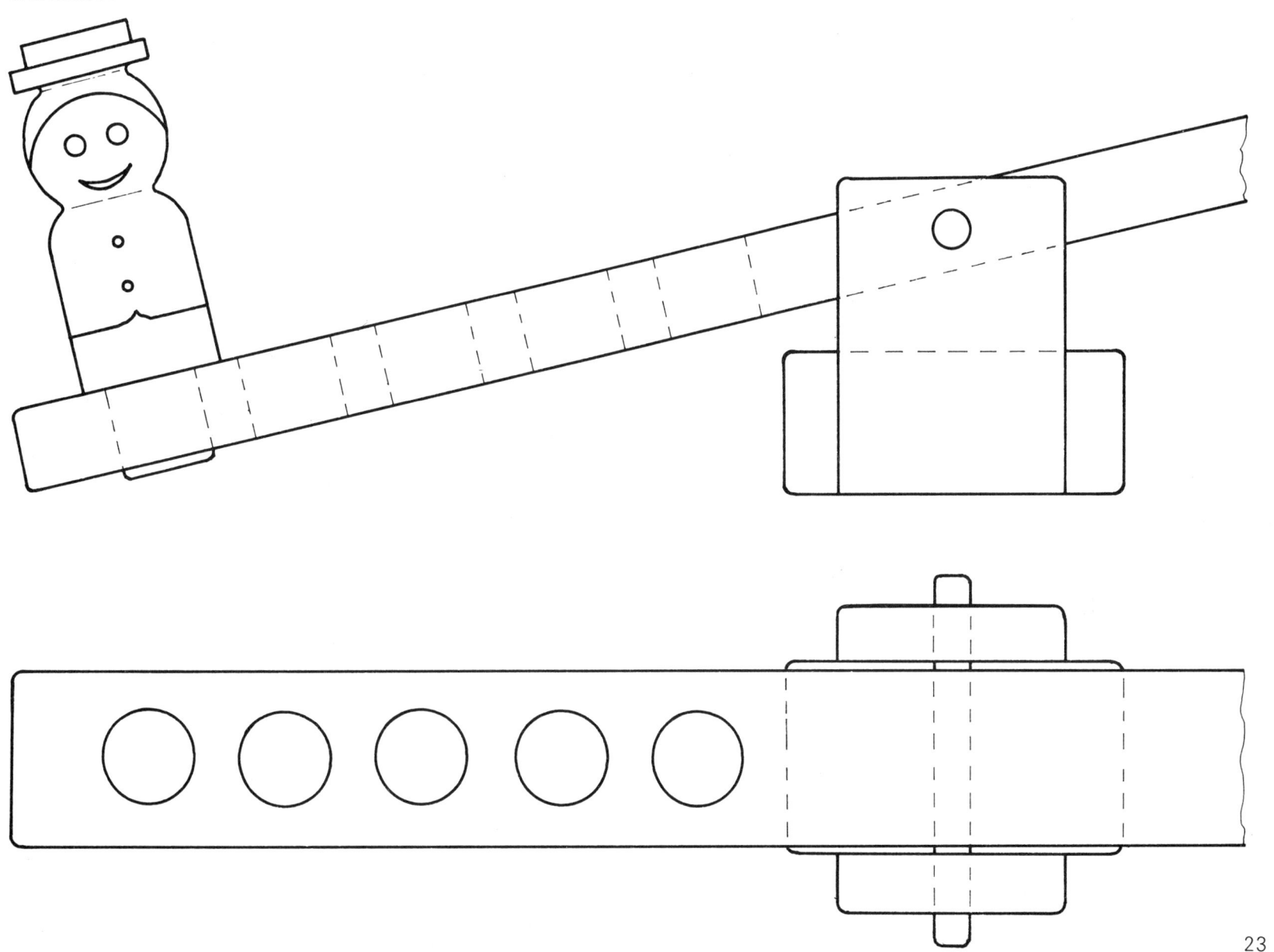

Seesaw

This is made from beech, although any wood can be used. The centre block is made from three pieces which are simply glued together and when set are drilled $\frac{1}{4}$" (6mm) to take a length of dowel. The centre hole in the long piece is drilled just over $\frac{1}{4}$" to provide an easy movement.

The figures shown were turned, although they could be shaped by hand from a piece of broom handle using rasps and files; in this case the hat could be omitted or a short piece of broom handle glued on. Likewise the peg bottom could be a short piece of dowel glued on or set in a hole in the base of the figure. The toy in the photograph was drilled only twice for the figures but it would make it more interesting if other holes were drilled, as in the drawing. If more figures were turned, then the distance between the holes would have to be increased. The axle should be lightly waxed with a piece of candle and carefully driven in with a hammer.

Stages in turning the figures:

1   Set the wood between centres. Turn to a cylinder.

2   Mark in the positions and turn, using a vee tool or skew chisel.

3   Round and smooth with tools and glass or garnet paper.

4   Reduce as required with a flat scraper turning tool.

5   Part off, using a parting tool, in the order a, b, c; and finally separate out of the lathe with a dovetail saw.

Finish with glasspaper and paint with bright colours. For painting, see page 96.

Seesaw

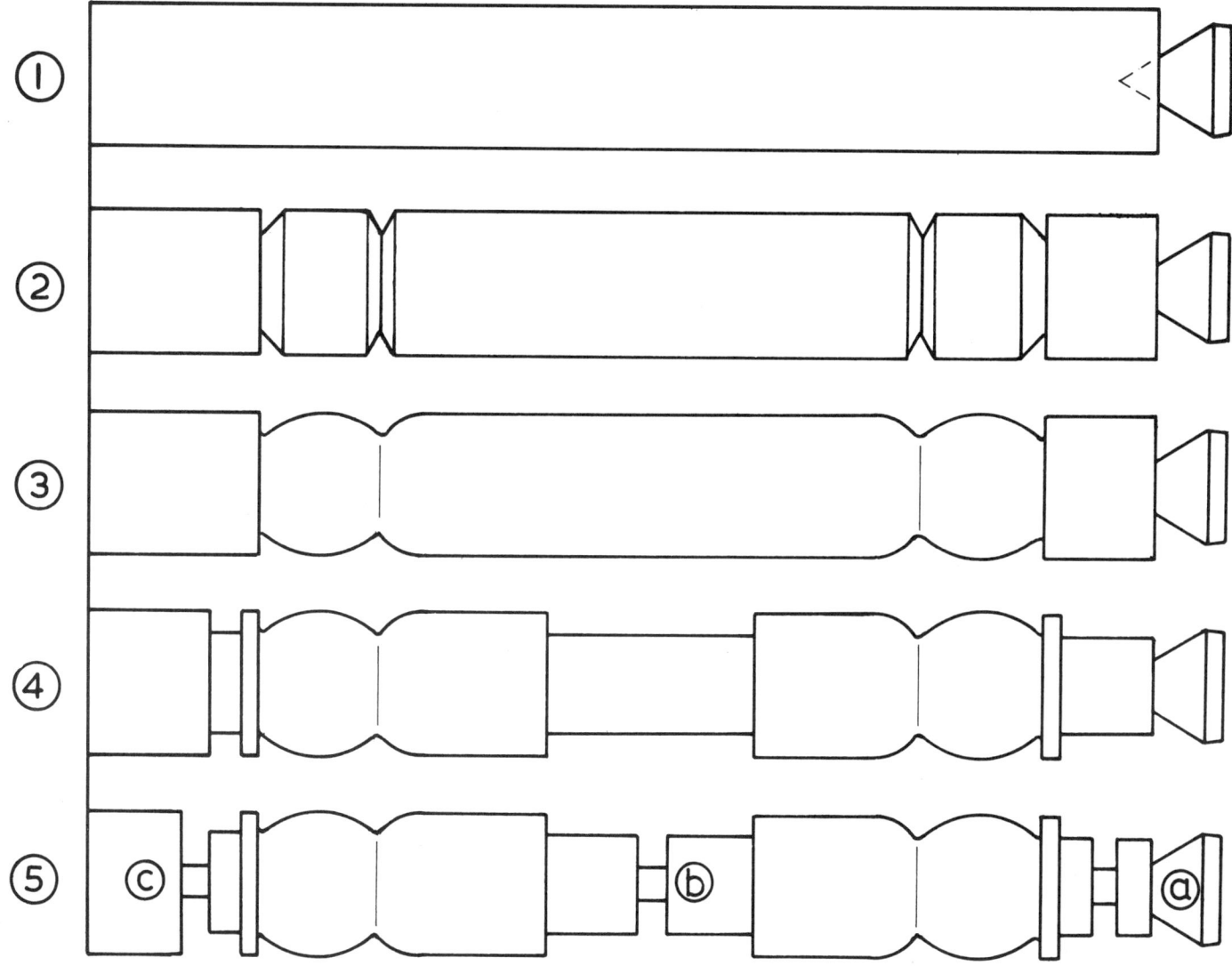

Windmill 1

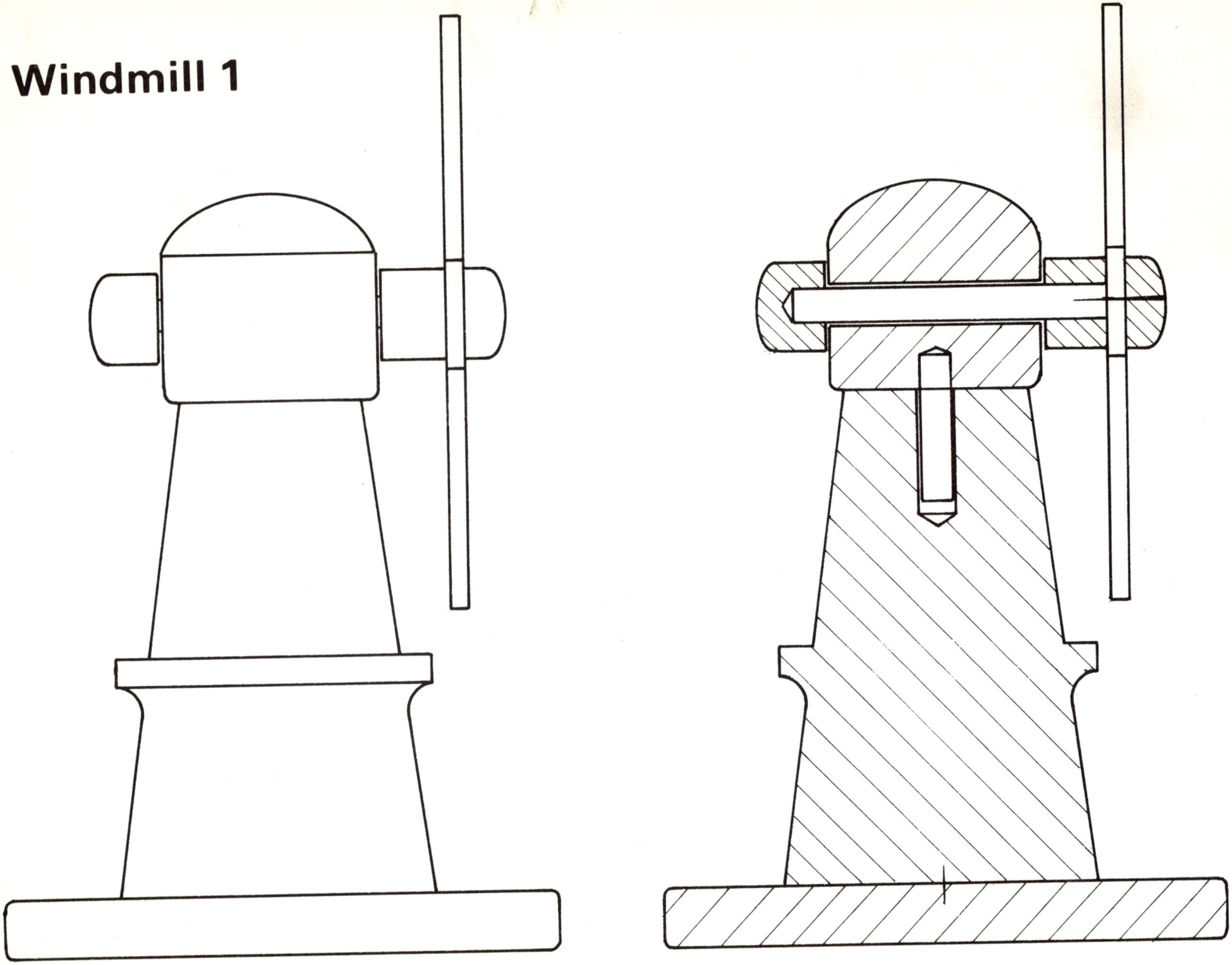

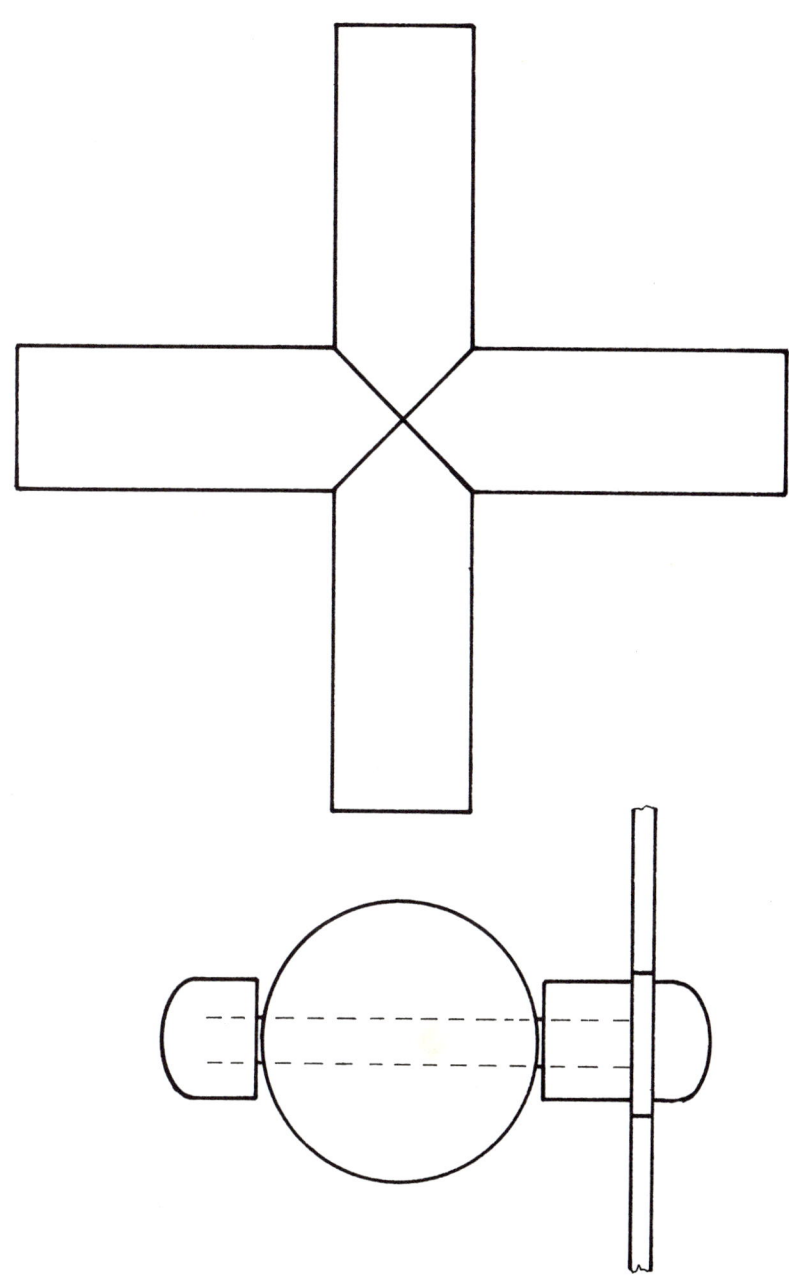

Windmill 1

This attractive toy can be turned from beech, or any wood that can be worked to a reasonable finish on a lathe. A windmill can also be made without a lathe (see Windmill 2). The top of the mill revolves on a $\frac{1}{4}''$ (6mm) dowel which is glued into the top but is free to spin in an oversize hole in the body. Alternatively, the top and body can be glued together on to a turned base. The sails are made from $\frac{1}{8}'' \times \frac{3}{4}''$ (3×20mm) material and are mitred at the centres. For an alternative form of sail, see page 31.

A piece of $\frac{1}{4}''$ dowel is used for the sail shaft; this is glued into a short piece of $\frac{5}{8}''$ (16mm) dowel, which can be drilled before being parted off on the lathe. A button of the same material can be nailed (veneer pin) to keep the sails in place while they are being glued into position. The dowel should be waxed (candle) before being passed through the oversize hole in the head. The whole assembly is then locked in place with a drilled button of $\frac{5}{8}''$ dowel, which is glued on to the end of the $\frac{1}{4}''$ dowel. If any of the parts are going to be painted, this is easier to do before the assembly of the parts. For painting, see page 96.

Windmill 1

Turning operations:

1 (Not illustrated.) Set the wood between centres and turn to a cylinder. The wood can also be set in a cup chuck, or ring chuck.

2 Turn the profile between centres. Clean to a finish.

3 Part deeply into the wood, starting at the tail stock end; but leave enough strength so that all partings and facings can be made—between centres.

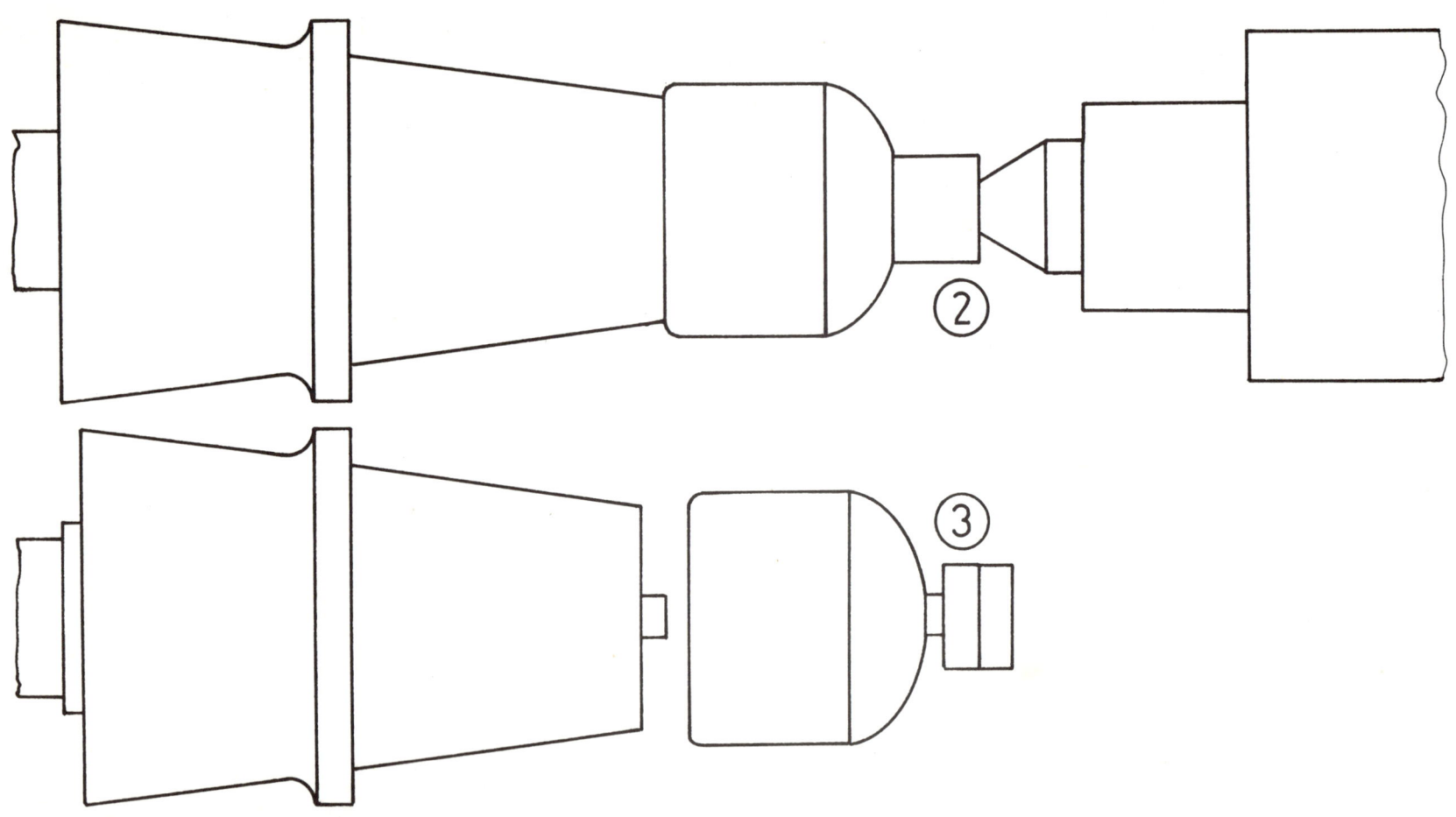

Windmill 1

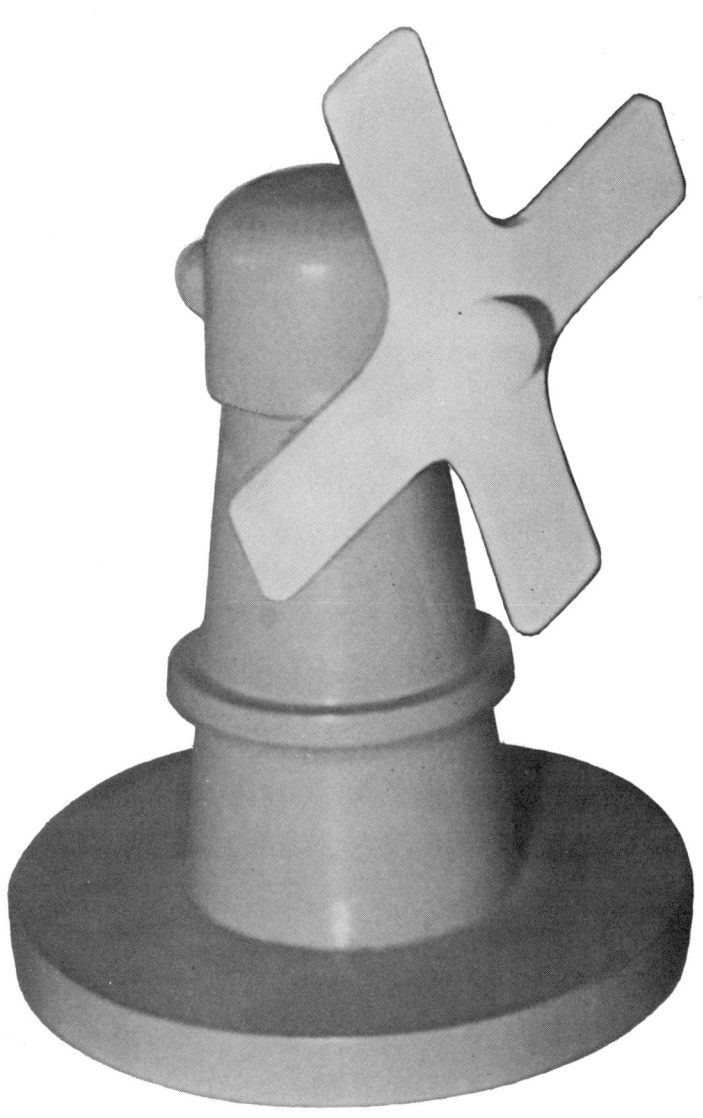

Windmill 2

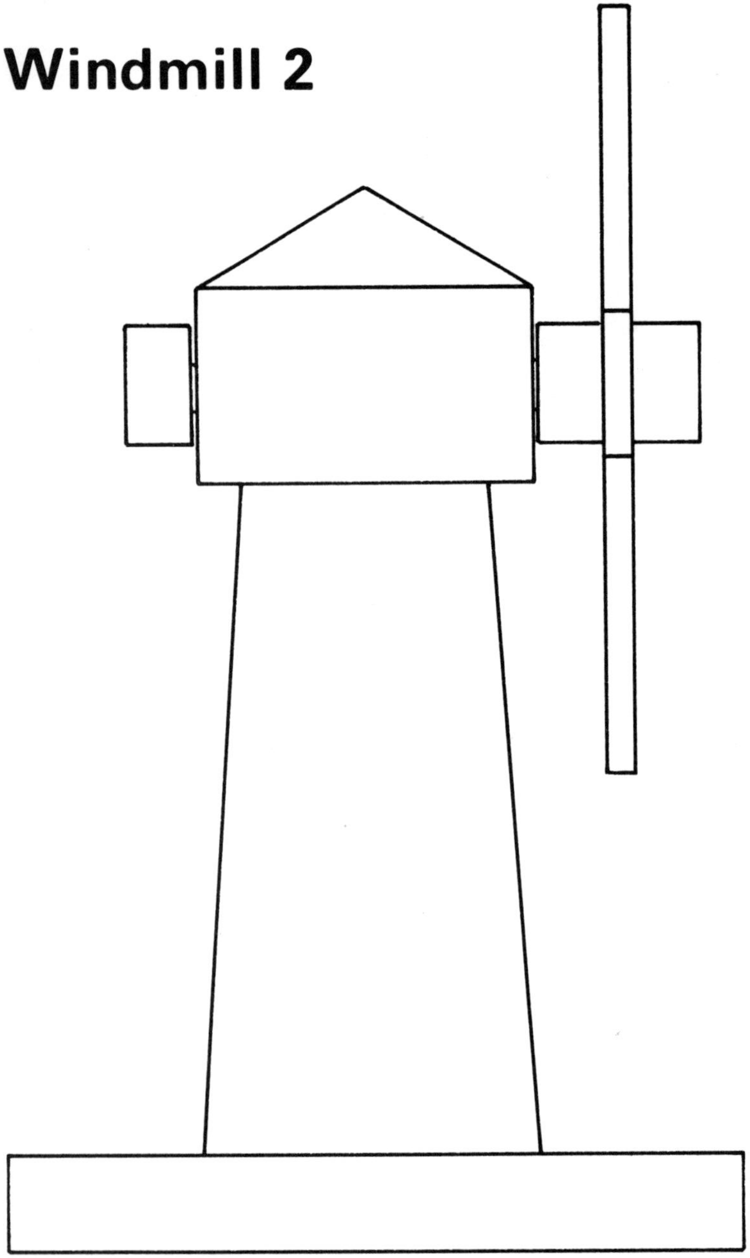

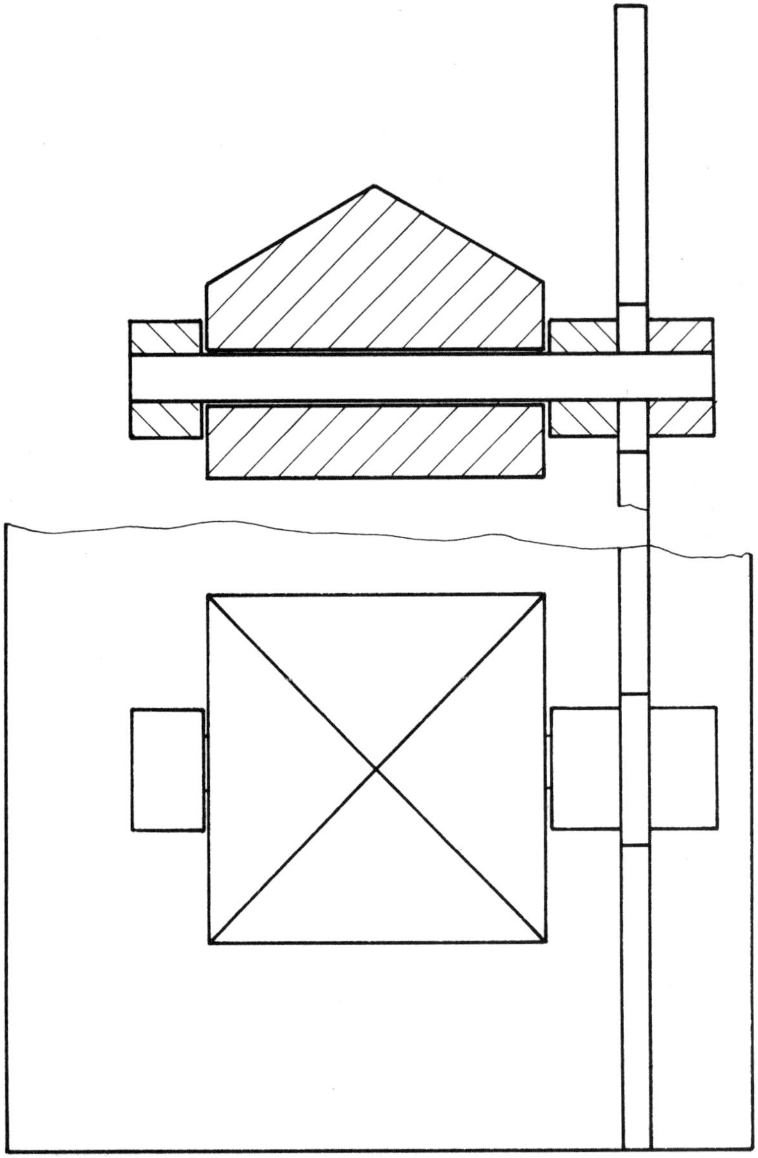

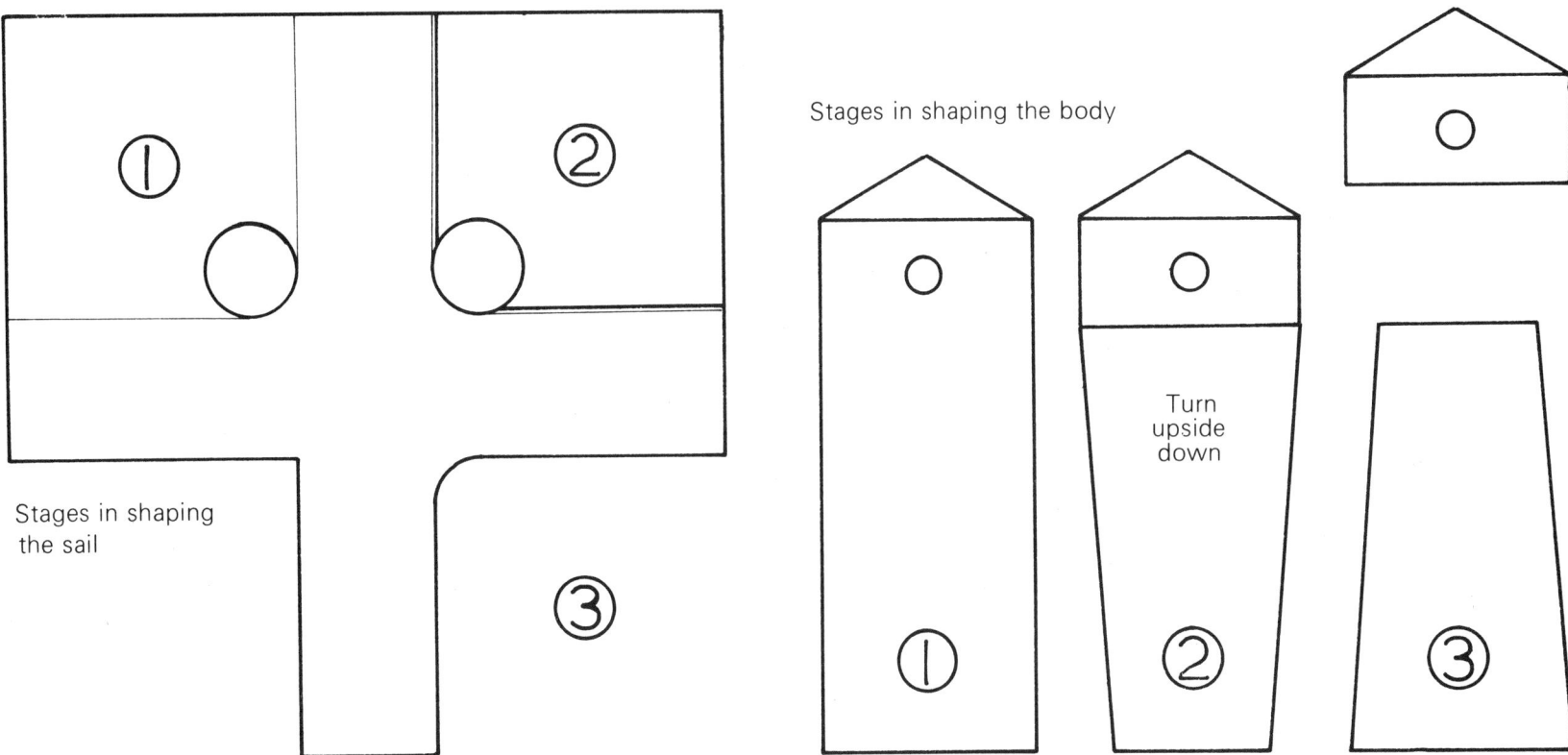

Stages in shaping the body

Turn upside down

Stages in shaping the sail

Windmill 2

This windmill is made from square section material 2″ (50mm) sawn, which will be rather less when planed. If the top and the body are left as one piece then the angles of the roof will be easier to cut. Likewise the hole $\frac{5}{16}$″ (7mm) for the sail dowel $\frac{1}{4}$″ (6mm is easier to drill when the two pieces are left together. Even the taper on the body can be made before the pieces are separated by sawing through. The head is glued to the body, which is then glued to the square base. The sail is cut from 3 or 4mm ply; the method of drilling out the corners gives an interesting appearance, although the corners could be sawn square. The sail is secured to the $\frac{1}{4}$″ dowel with three slices of drilled $\frac{5}{8}$″ (16mm) dowel. Remember to glue the last piece of dowel after the 'axle' has been passed through the head. The sail should now be free to revolve; this is made easy if some candle wax is applied where necessary, and not where gluing is to take place. The toy can be left as plain wood or varnished. Parts can be painted (see page 96). A coloured body and top with a plain or white sail will look attractive. It is better to finish the painting before the sail assembly is finally glued into position.

Large Removal Van

This sturdy toy can be sat on, as well as pulled along. It is a toy that a 2- to 3-year-old will really enjoy. The loading and unloading through the drop end will add to the pleasure. The body, apart from the top, $\frac{1}{4}''$ (6mm) ply, is made from $\frac{1}{2}''$ (12mm) blockboard. This was chosen because it can easily be glued and nailed together, and does make the toy really strong. The side

of the cabin is cut out from the side of the van. Later, after assembly, the cut-out is glued into position inside the van. The cut-out from the rear wheel is not used again, but the space is filled with a rectangle of ply. The plastic wheels are set on $\frac{1}{4}''$ (6mm) steel axle, which can be bought with the wheels and hub caps. The two housings (grooves) for the axles are cut into

Large Removal Van

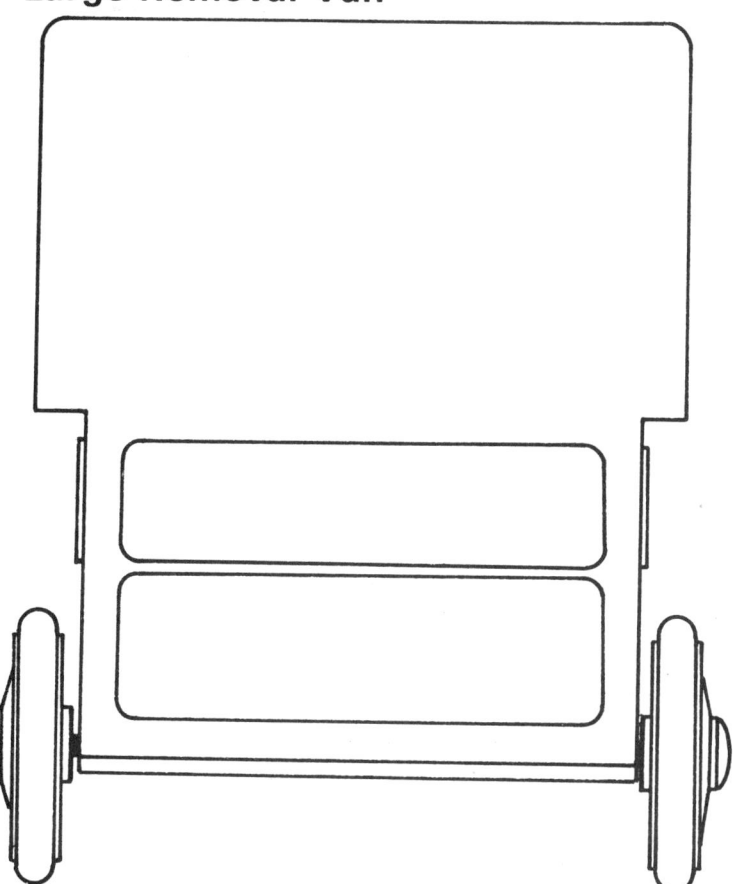

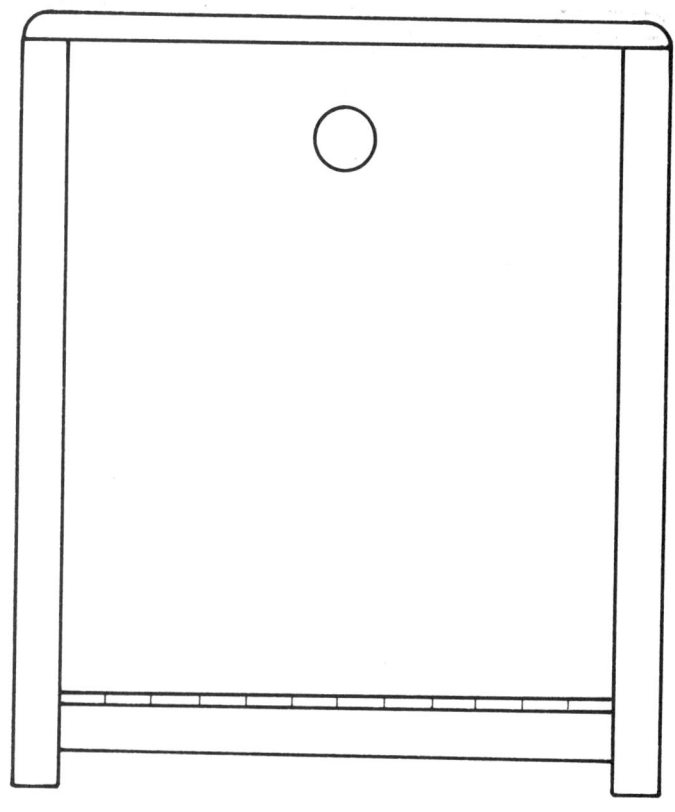

the underside of the bottom of the van; this operation is best done before the assembly of the van. The drop-down back has a $\frac{5}{8}''$ (15mm) finger-hole drilled through, and is hinged for the whole of its length with a piece of heavy piano hinge. The windows are made from white Formica and the bonnet front is a piece of ply that is glued and nailed on. When attractively painted (see page 96) this will be a first-class toy.

C

Large Removal Van

Large Removal Van

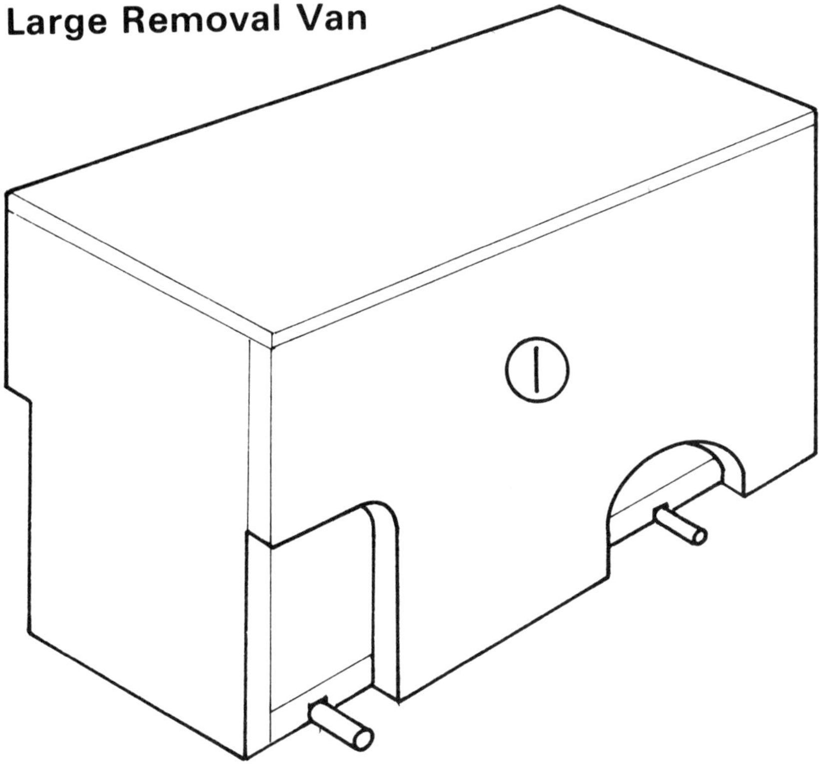

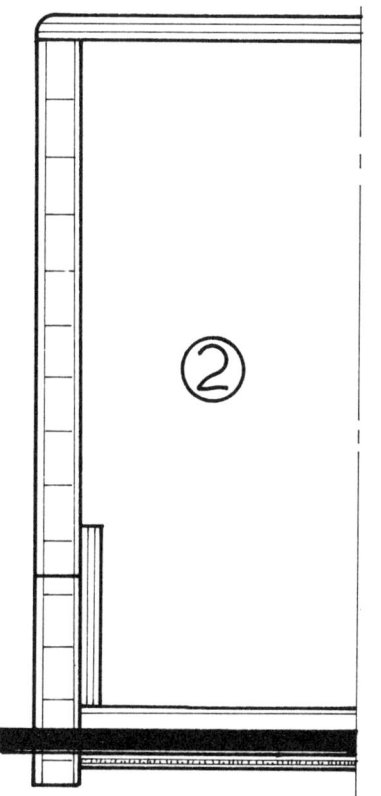

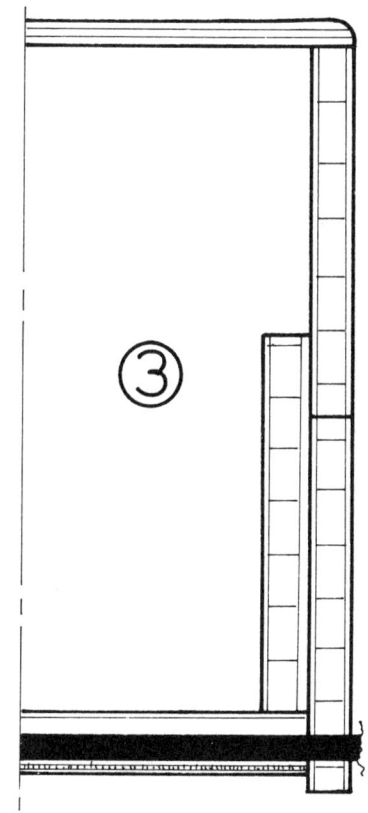

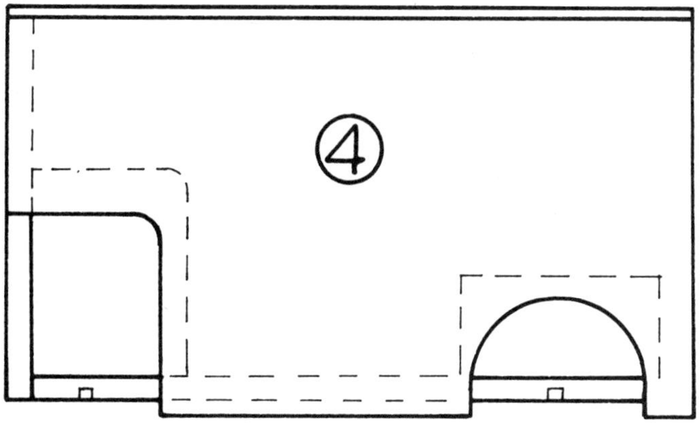

1 General view of the assembly
2 Half section through rear wheel arch
3 Half section through cabin and wheel arch
4 Side, showing cutouts. The front cutout is used to infill the cabin side. The back cutout is infilled with ply.

Rocking Hen

Rocking Hen

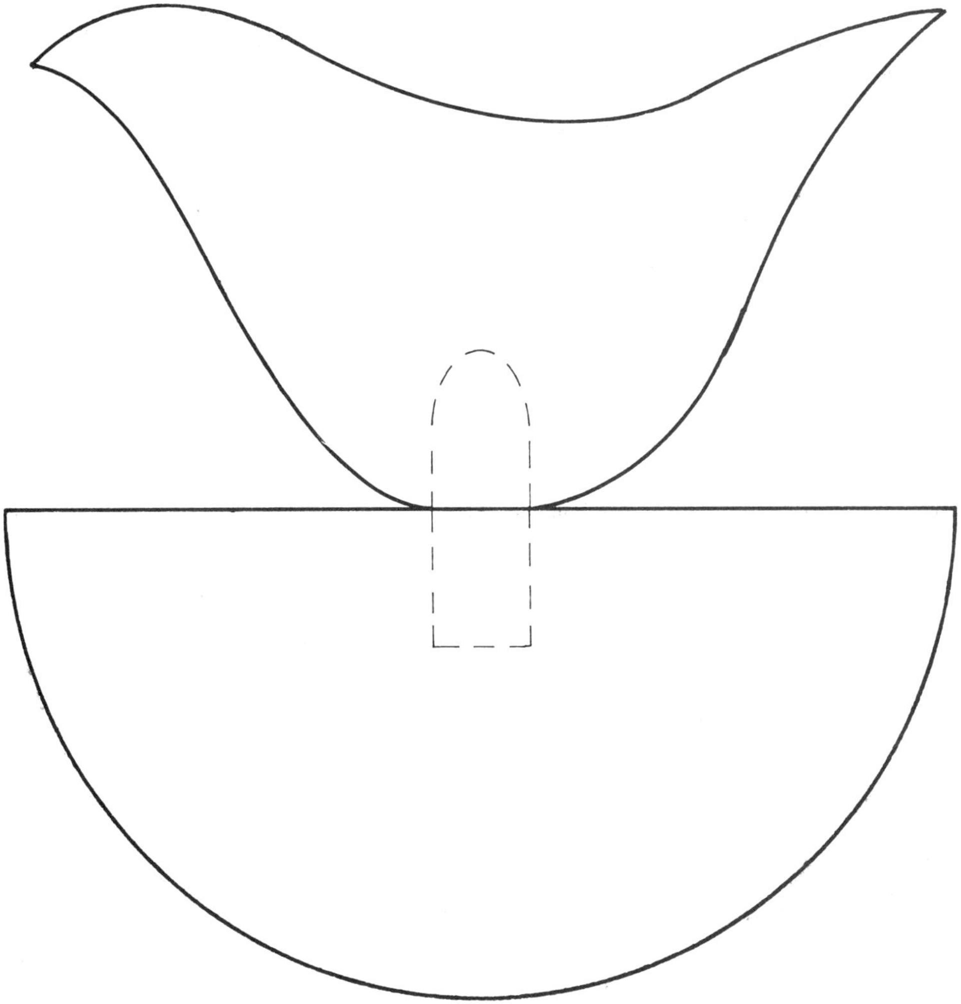

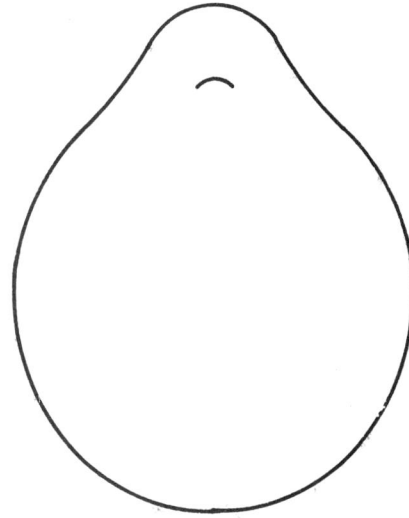

This could be a toy to amuse anyone—even an executive. Some say it rocks, some say it feeds; this is a debatable point.

The base is turned from the solid, and the screw holes made in securing it to a face plate are filled with hard filler. The hen is sculpted from the solid wood; a holding block can be glued on and left until the sculpting is nearly complete. This makes the shaping operations much easier. The hen is set on a $\frac{1}{2}''$ (12mm) dowel which is glued into the rocker and the hen can be removed from this peg. The base is painted (see page 96).

The idea can be adapted for making rocking animals; some suggested shapes are given on page 39.

Rocking Hen

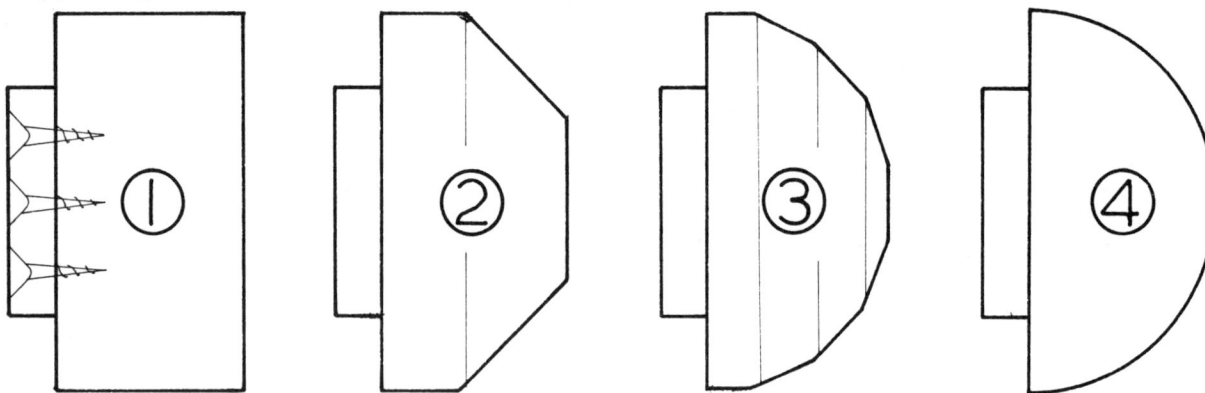

Stages in turning the base

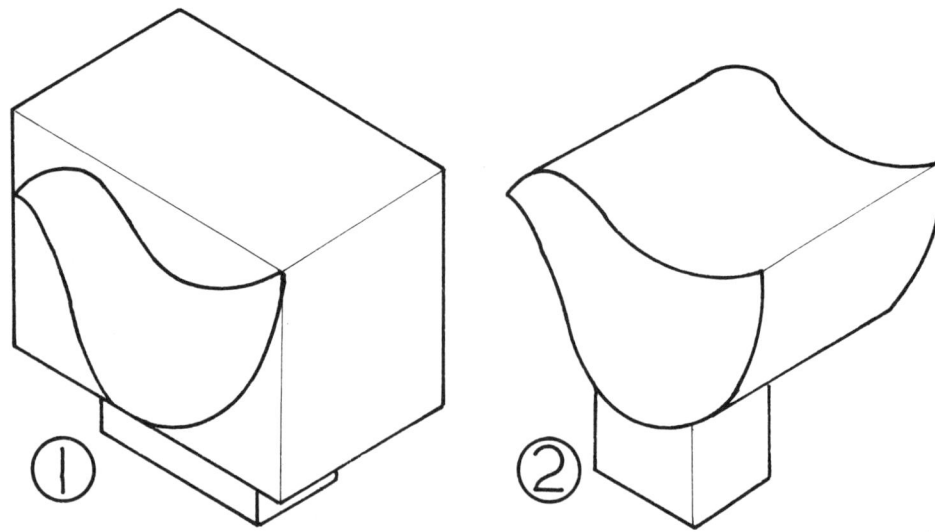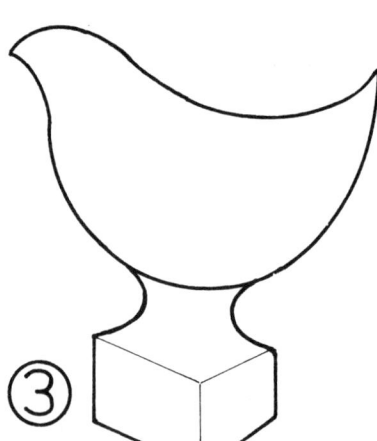

Stages in sculpting the hen

Rocking Animals

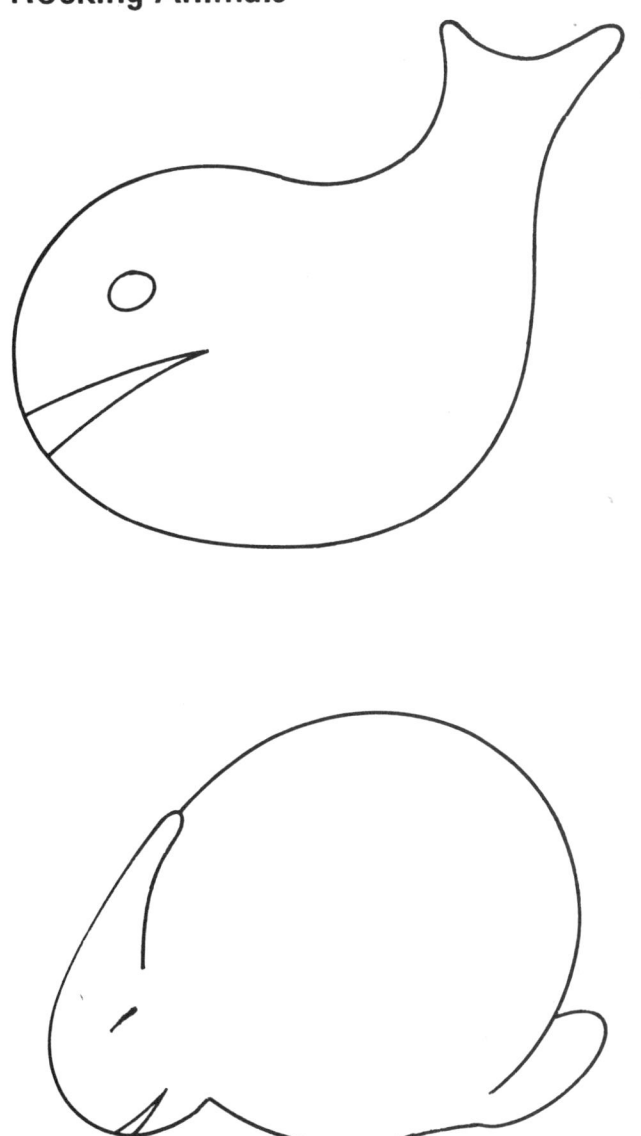

Pocket Solitaire

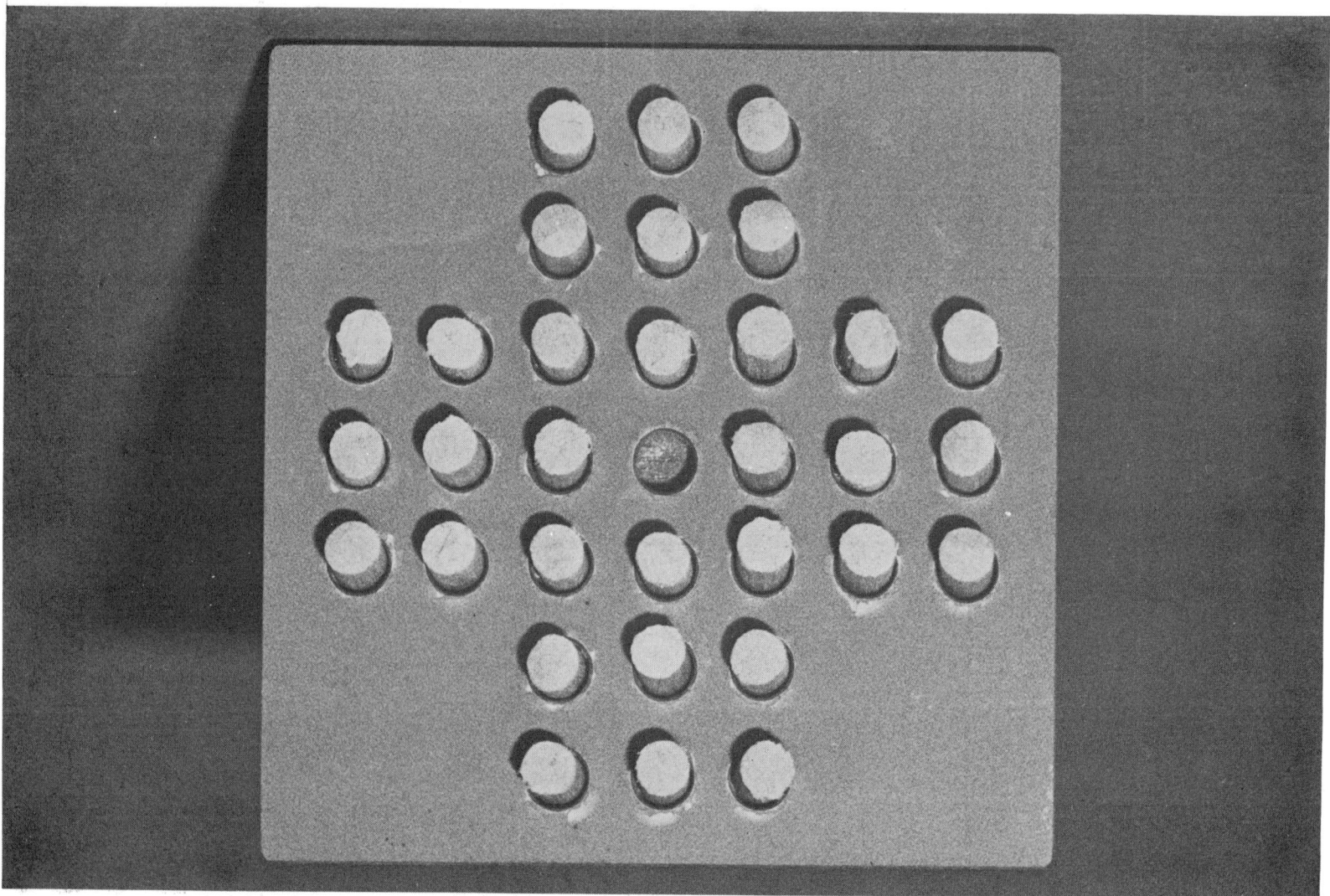

Pocket Solitaire

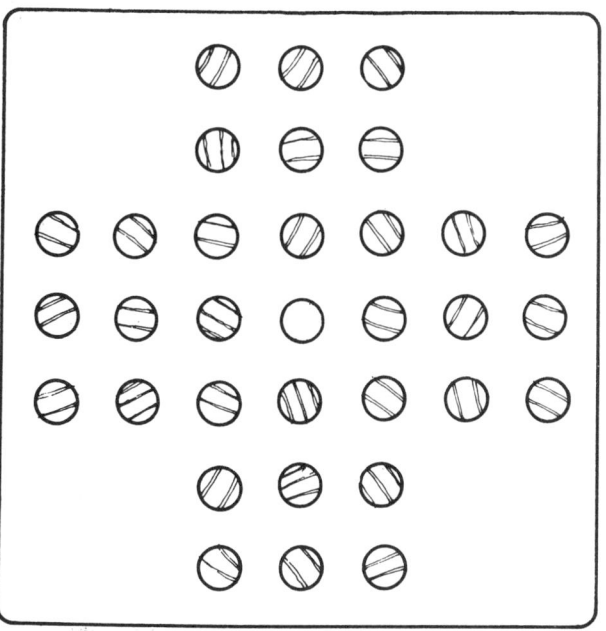

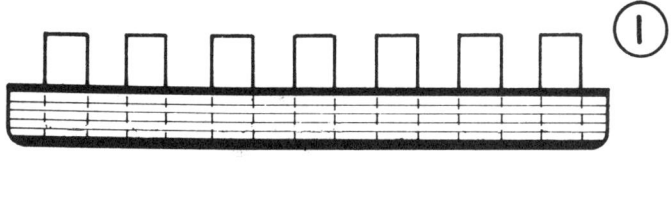

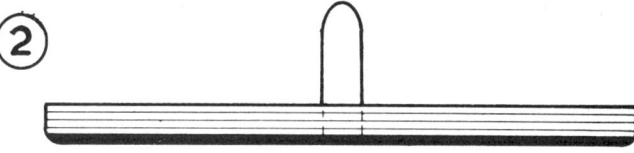

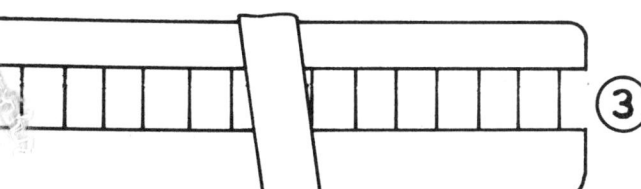

1   The peg board with pegs
2   The cover with central peg
3   The board and cover closed and fastened together
     with a tight rubber band, for carrying in the pocket.

Pocket Solitaire

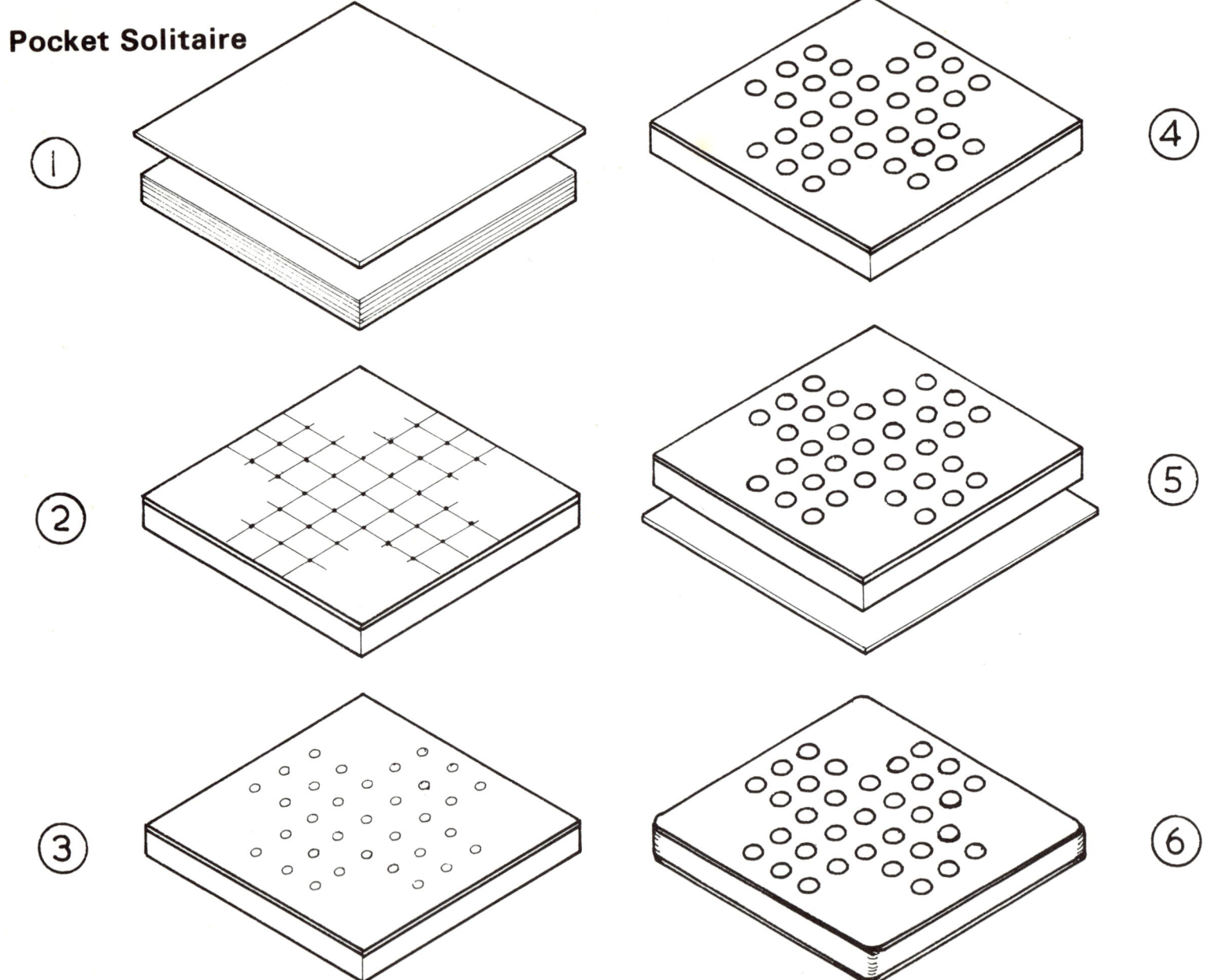

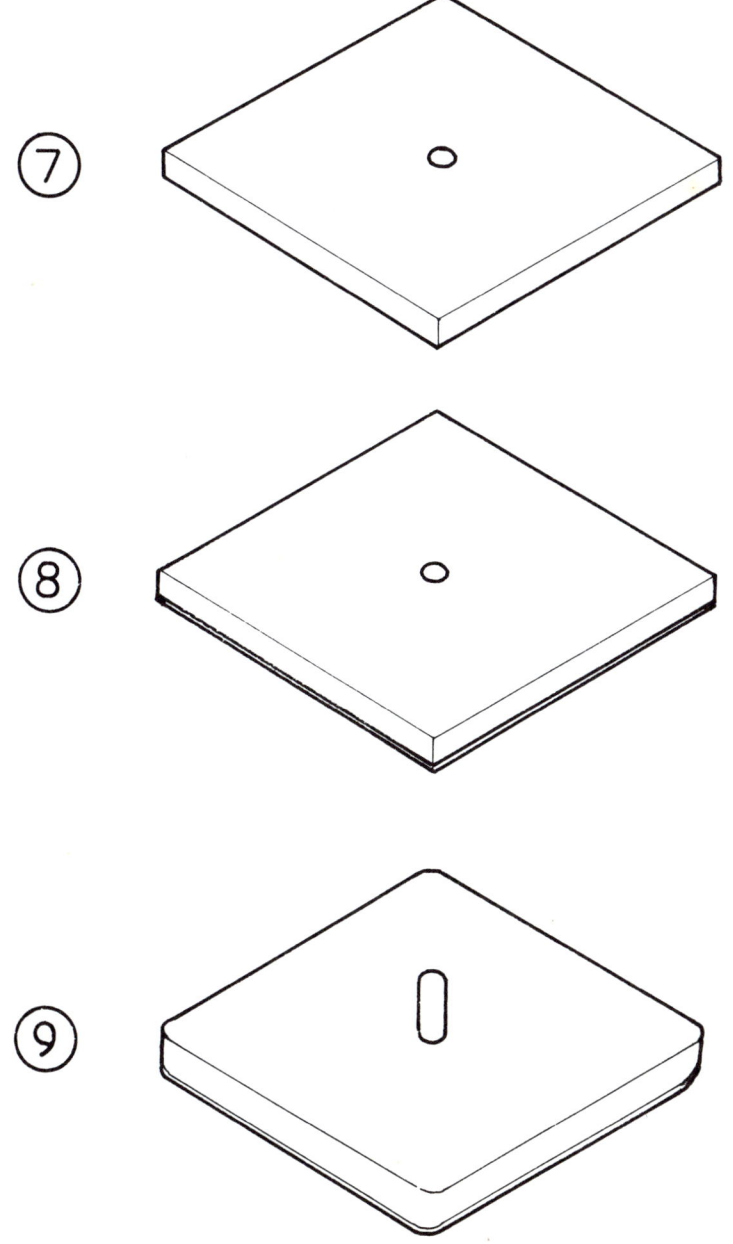

Pocket Solitaire

1 Prepare a 3¾″ (95mm) square of 6mm ply and a slightly larger piece of plastic laminate (Formica, etc.) and glue together.

2 Trim the edges of the plastic laminate and mark in the lines with a sharp pencil. Stab in with a scriber or very lightly centre punch the hole positions.

3 Drill about half way through the wood with a ⅛″ (3mm) drill.

4 Drill through with a $\frac{9}{32}$″ (7.5mm) drill—slightly over a ¼″ (6mm) for ¼″ dowel pegs.

5 To cover the drilling blemishes on the under side, glue on another piece of plastic laminate.

6 Generally clean the edges and round the corners.

7 Prepare a piece of 4mm ply to a square 3¾″ (95mm) and drill a ¼″ hole in the centre to take a piece of ¼″ dowel.

8 Glue on a piece of plastic laminate and trim to a square.

9 Round the edges and corners and glue in a piece of ¼″ dowel (test for length when the pegs are in position). The peg should enter the unoccupied centre hole of the peg board.

Now cut 36 (4 spare) pieces of ¼″ dowel to ⅝″ (15mm) in length (Sawing Block, page 94). Clean the ends on a glasspaper board (page 95). This can be done when all the pegs are in place. They are placed in the peg board, leaving the centre hole empty. Finally the cover is fitted on. All the parts are held in place with a tight rubber band.

Table Solitaire

Table Solitaire

A larger board can be made from a thick piece of wood (page 44) approximately 8″–9″ square (200–230mm) × 1″ (25mm). The holes can be drilled $\frac{1}{2}$″–$\frac{5}{8}$″ (12–15mm) in diameter, and the pegs can be made from square stick with the corners removed.

How to play solitaire

Place a peg in every hole except for the centre. To play, remove all the pegs from the board except for one, which must be in the centre hole. Pegs are removed from the board one at a time, by jumping one peg over another into a vacant space immediately beyond. Pegs can be moved vertically and horizontally, but not diagonally.

Square peg in a round hole

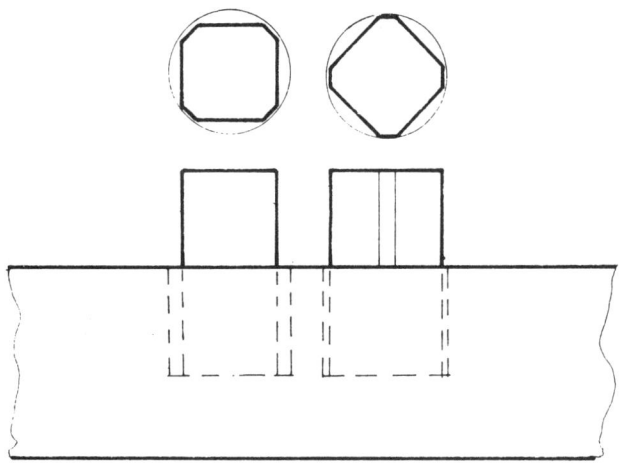

Circular form for table or pocket boards

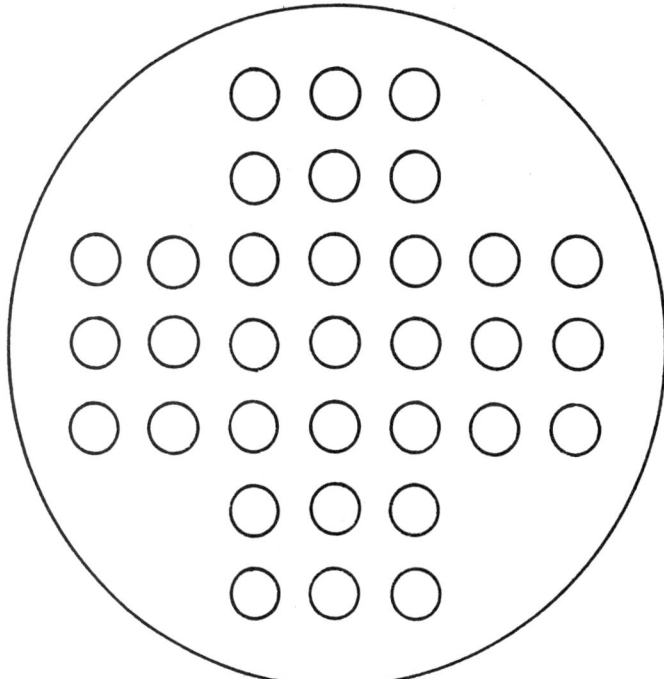

45

Helicopter

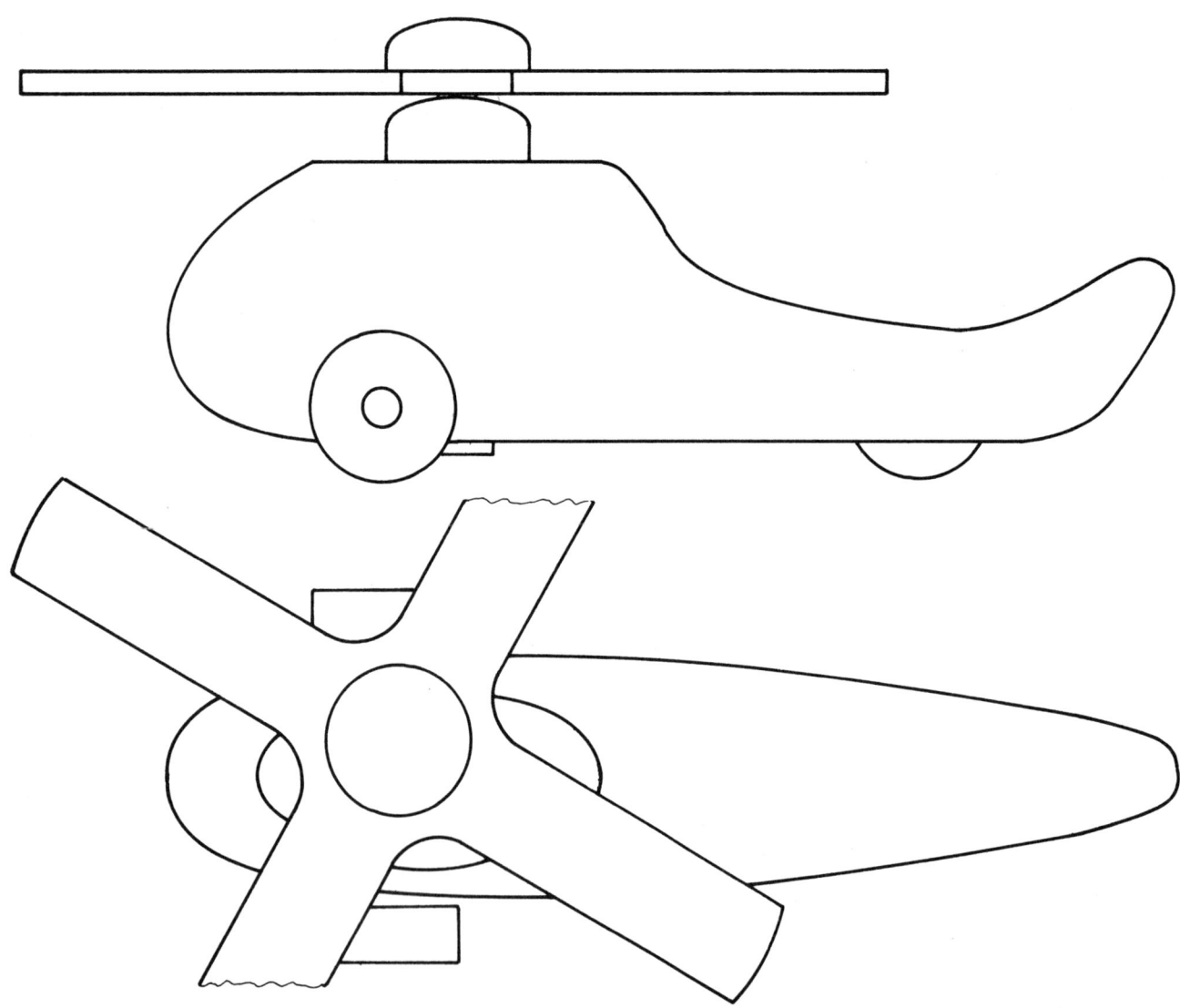

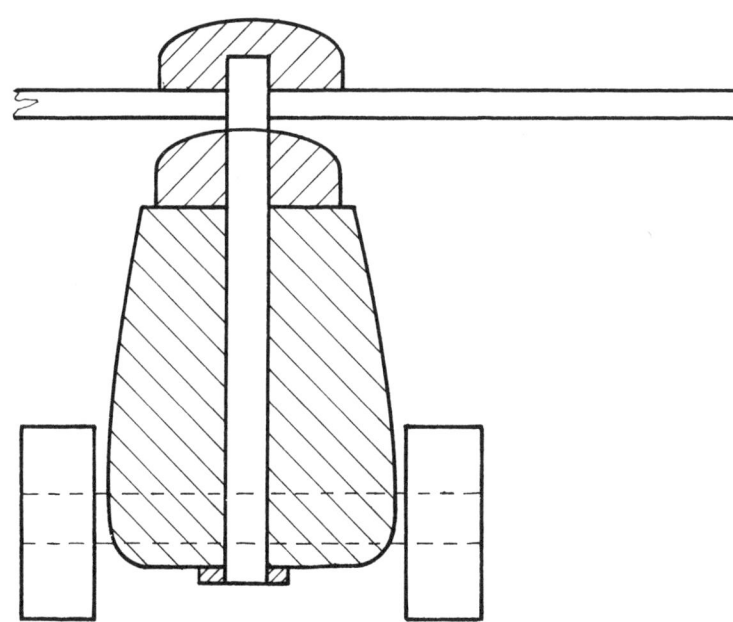

Helicopter

This is an attractive sturdy toy that can be pulled along and the propeller spun round. A piece of soft wood can be used for the body, although of course some hardwoods are easy or even easier to work than some softwoods. It is essential to select a piece of wood that is longer than the body so that it can be held in a vice until nearly all the work is finished; then it can be cut from the holding piece for final working.

The outline from the top is marked on to the wood. As this shape is symmetrical it is a good idea to fold a piece of paper and mark only one half. This is cut with a pair of scissors, opened, folded flat and marked round on to the smooth top wood surface. It is important to drill two holes before any shaping is done. The propeller shaft and the axle are made from $\frac{1}{4}$" (6mm) dowel, so $\frac{5}{16}$" (8mm) drill holes will allow the dowel to turn freely, especially if some candle wax is applied to the surfaces.

The propeller is cut from 3 or 4mm ply (see page 31, Windmill). A boss is glued to the top of the propeller to increase the strength of the joint between the propeller and the shaft. There is another on top of the cabin. Both of these are pieces of broom handle (page 94) which have been rounded by hand or in a lathe; or they can be left square. The three wheels can also be cut from broom handle and drilled (pages 94, 95). After the wheel surfaces have been cleaned the dowel is glued into one, and the tail wheel (half) is glued on to the body.

Before any assembly of the parts the propeller, body and wheels should be painted if required (page 96). Make sure that when the propeller and its boss are glued to the shaft they are set nicely square. The shaft is then passed through the body, and a small disc of thin drilled ply is glued on to the underside of the shaft. Be careful with the glue; do not lock the whole lot solid. The wheel axle is now passed through its hole, and the second wheel glued and tapped into place.

Helicopter

Helicopter

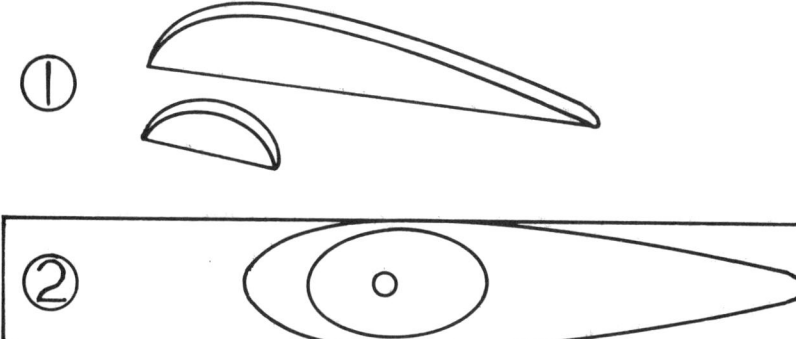

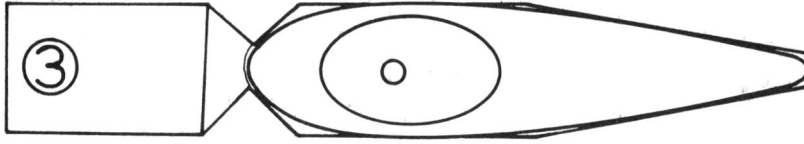

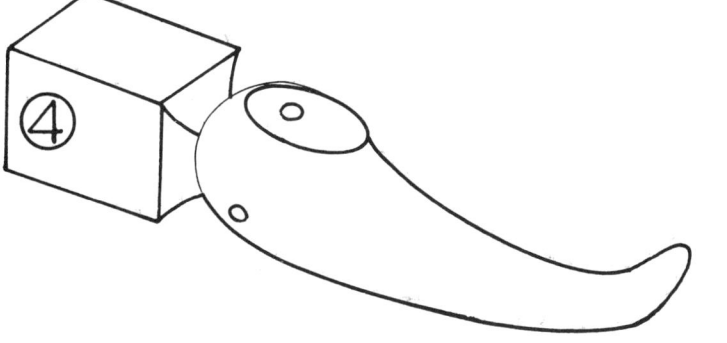

1 Folded paper shapes of top cut out.

2 Plan of outlines marked on wood. Two holes are drilled, one for the propeller shaft and other for the wheel axle.

3 Pieces are sawn off close to the outline, but the body is not separated from the block for holding in the vice.

4 The side view is drawn on and the shape cut with a coping saw. The general shaping is done with a spokeshave, surforms, rasps, and finally finished with various grades of glasspaper.

D

Jumbo Aeroplane

Jumbo Aeroplane

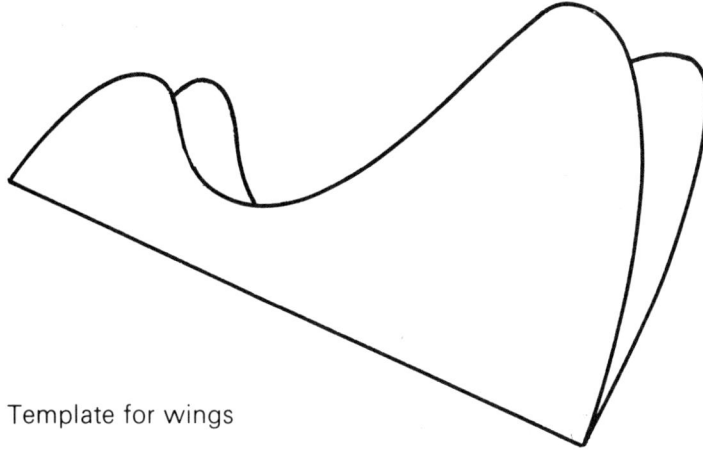

Template for wings

A half template (pattern) can be traced or freely drawn on a folded piece of paper and cut out with scissors.

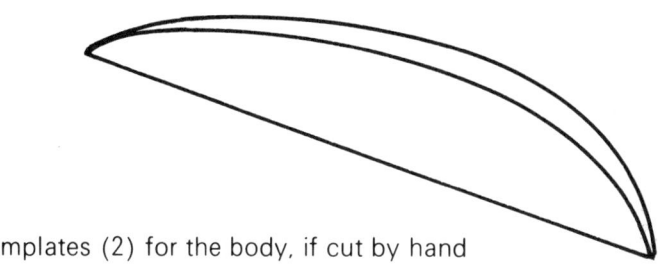

Templates (2) for the body, if cut by hand

This is a chunky toy that can be just buzzed around in the hand. The propeller can be rotated with a flick of the finger. It could be suspended on a nylon cord to amuse the baby or could form part of an aircraft collection together with other models in this book.

The wings are all made in one piece of plywood (3 or 4mm). The body (fuselage) of the toy was turned on a lathe, but it can also be shaped by hand. The body when turned is sawn down the middle. The sawing line can be marked in, using vee blocks and a gauge (before the centre ends are cut off). Much more simply, if a strip of paper is rolled round the widest part and the measurement halved, this can be transferred to the body and the centre line can then be marked in from centre to the tips with a flexible steel ruler and pencil (four separate lines).

When the body has been sawn through the top half is slotted with a saw to take the rudder, made from 4mm ply. The two halves of the body can be glued to the wings. The first half can be nailed in position through the ply, and this will prevent both pieces from skidding around when glued and pressed into position. When the glue is set the plane is stood on its end and a $\frac{1}{4}$'' (6mm) hole drilled for the propeller assembly (see the illustrations). The propeller is cut from 4mm ply with a fret-saw. A spot of glue is dropped into the $\frac{1}{4}$'' hole and the propeller is threaded on to the nose dowel for gluing in.

Painting has not yet been mentioned. The model shown was painted (page 96) with bright yellow, with the propeller in white. This makes a very attractive model.

Jumbo Aeroplane

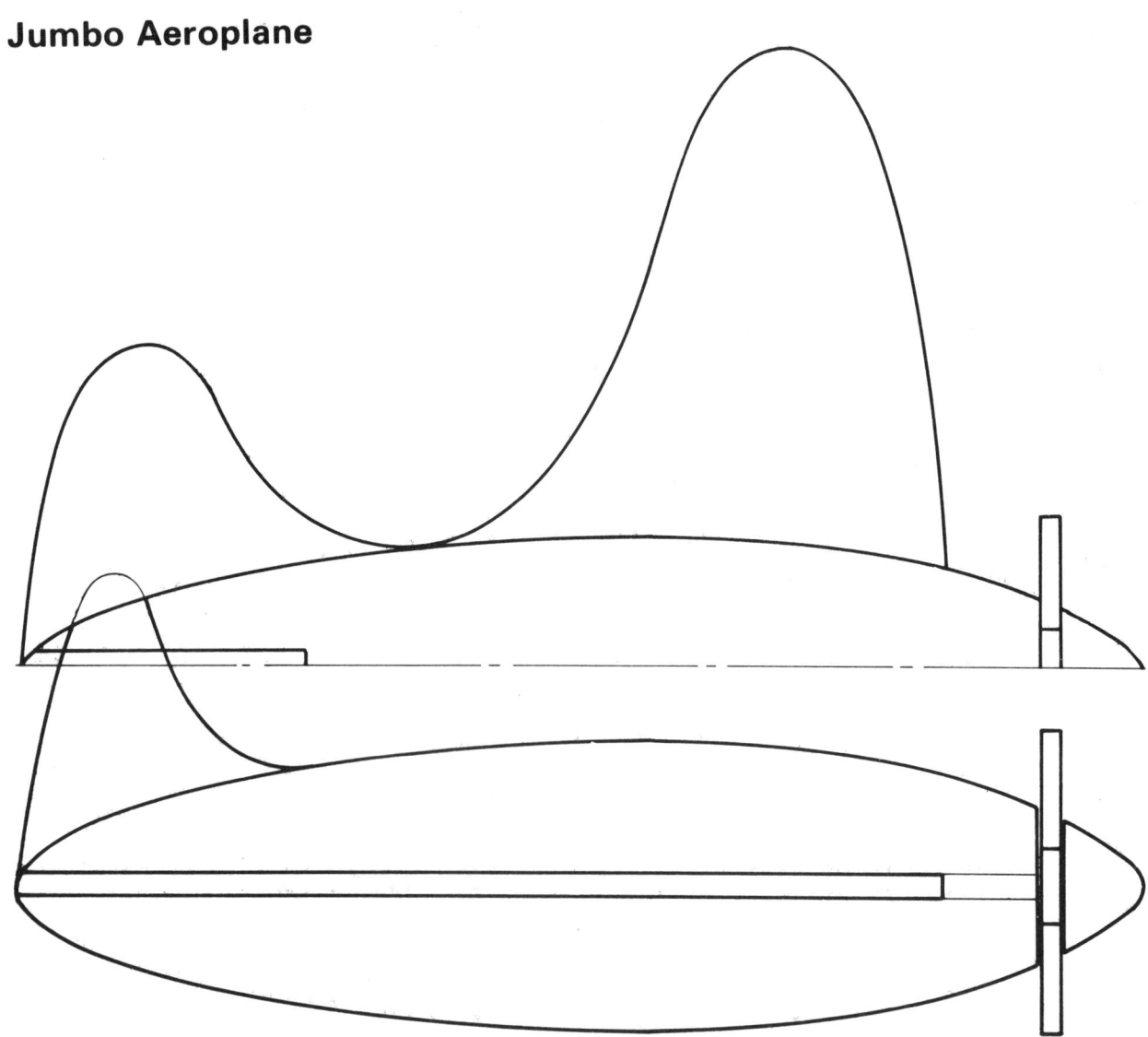

Jumbo Aeroplane

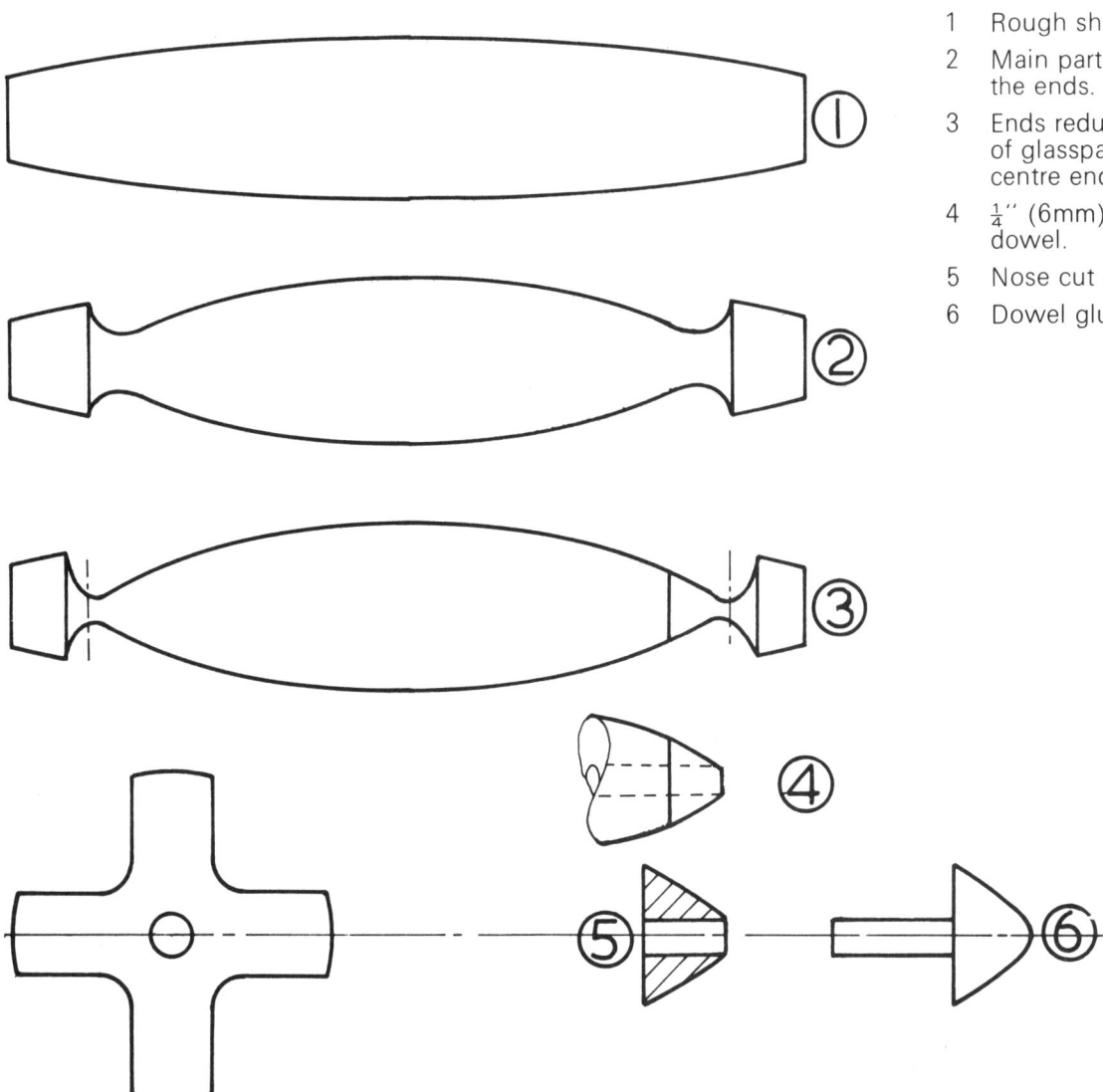

Turning operations

1 Rough shaping between centres.
2 Main part of the body finished and necked in at the ends.
3 Ends reduced further and all finished with grades of glasspaper. Mark in the nose. Cut off body from centre ends.
4 $\frac{1}{4}''$ (6mm) hole drilled in nose end for propeller dowel.
5 Nose cut off carefully with a fine saw.
6 Dowel glued in nose.

Jumbo Aeroplane

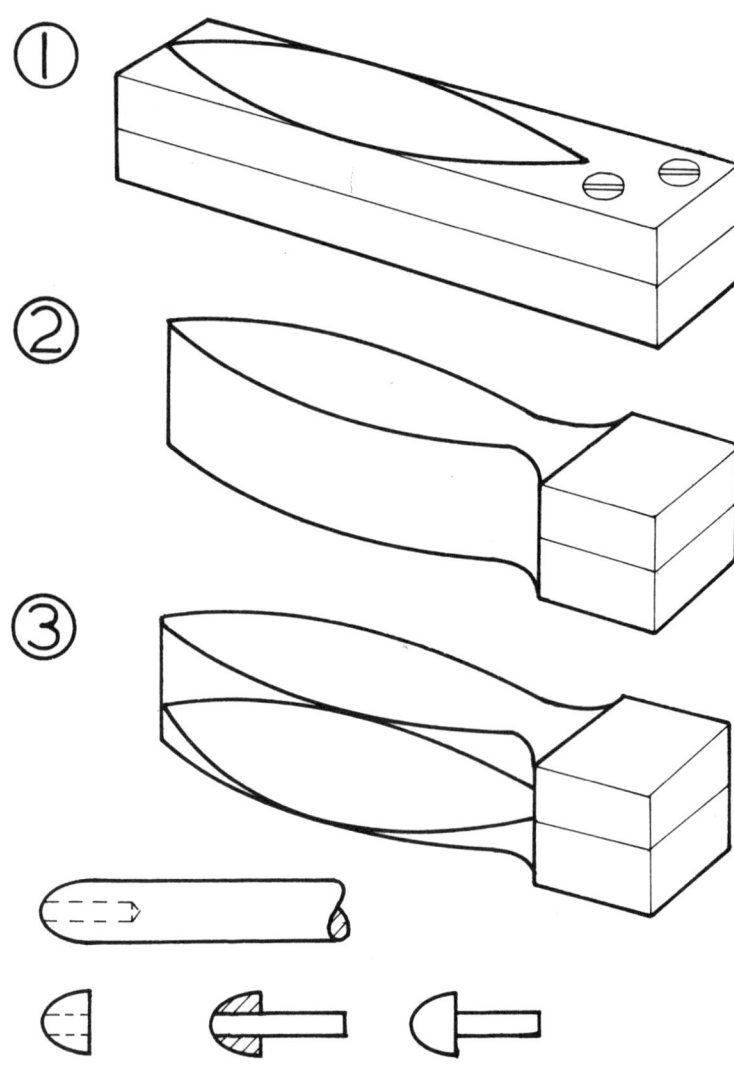

The nose can be made from dowel.

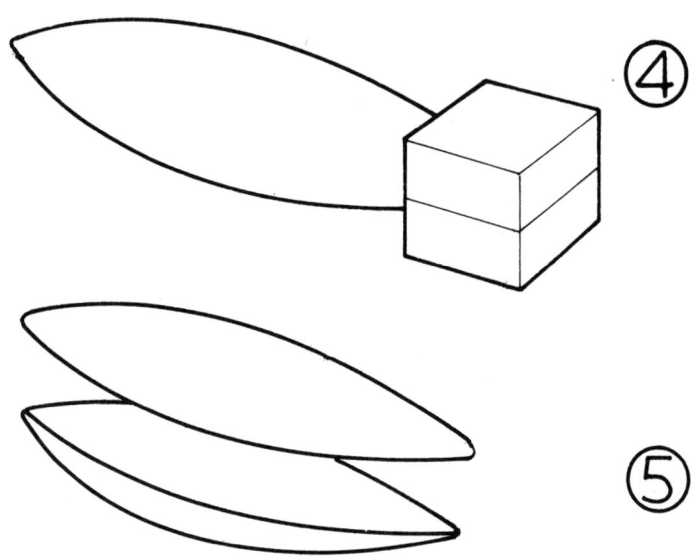

Shaping the body by hand:

1 Two blocks screwed together at one end, and plan marked in using paper template.

2 Cut and shaped to plan outline.

3 Side view marked in using paper template; some adjustment may be necessary.

4 Cut to outline and fully rounded, using saw, spokeshave, surform tools, rasps and grades of glasspaper.

5 Body halves separated from the screw block and finished off.

Counting Frame

Counting Frame

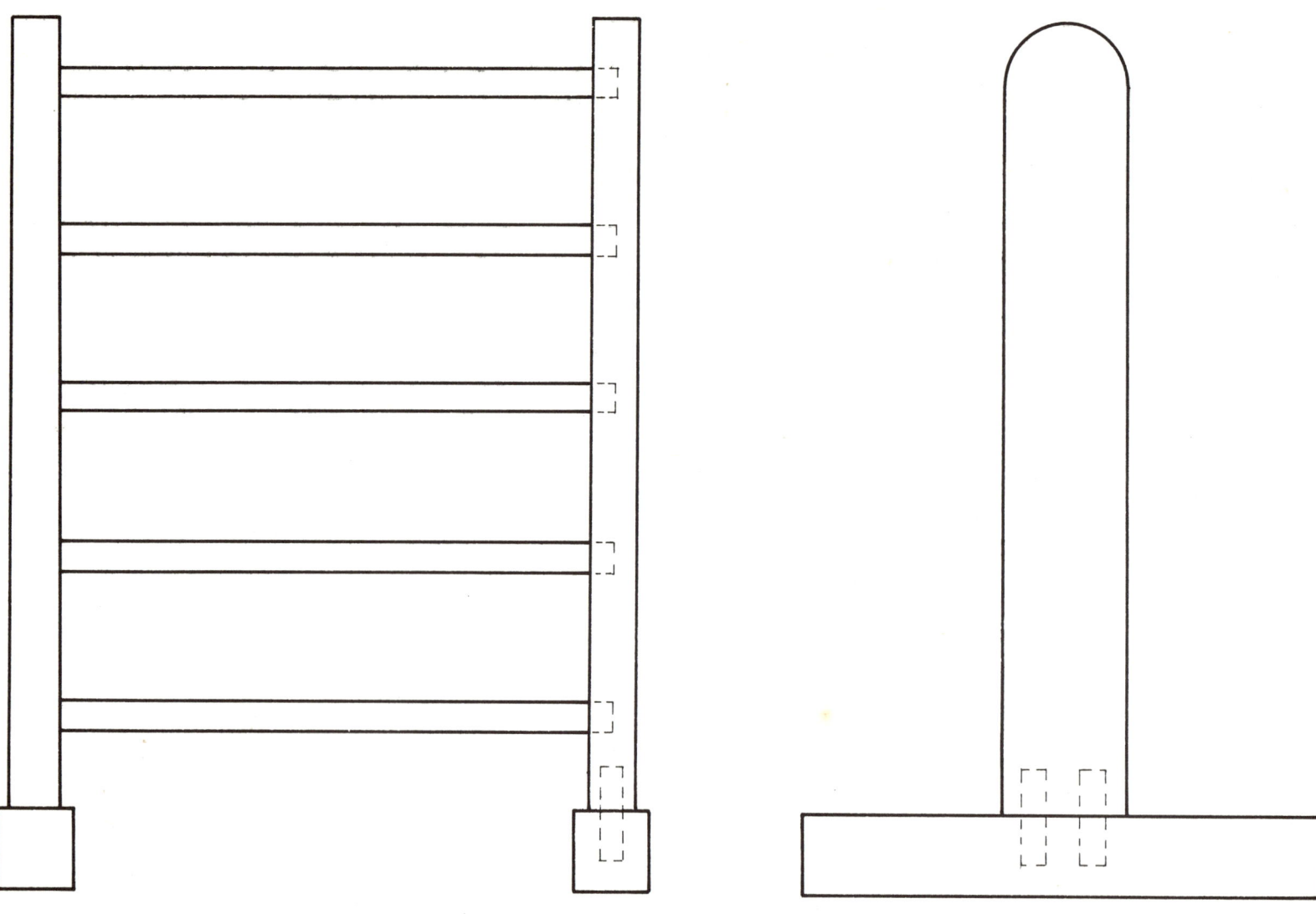

Counting Frame

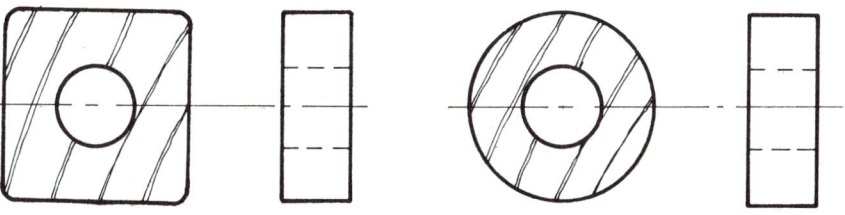

This is a sturdy toy and simple to make; it can be used in the upright or inclined position. It is made from beech, but most woods would be suitable. The overall width is 8½" (215mm) and the overall height is 10¾" (270mm). The uprights are made from 1⅝" × ⅝" (40 × 15mm), and the feet are cut from 1" (25mm) square material. The five ⅜" (9mm) dowels are 7½" (190mm) long, and the ⅜" thick counters are cut from 1" (25mm) square material; and these are drilled slightly over ⅜". Alternatively the counters could be drilled and cut from 1" wide strips of three-ply. The uprights are joined to the feet by two dowels. It is easier to paint or stain the counters before lightly gluing the dowels into the side frames. For painting, see page 96.

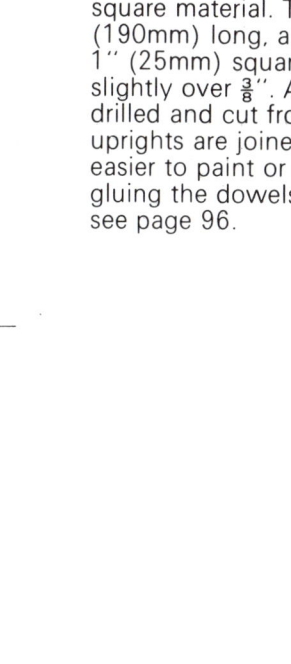

Counting Rod

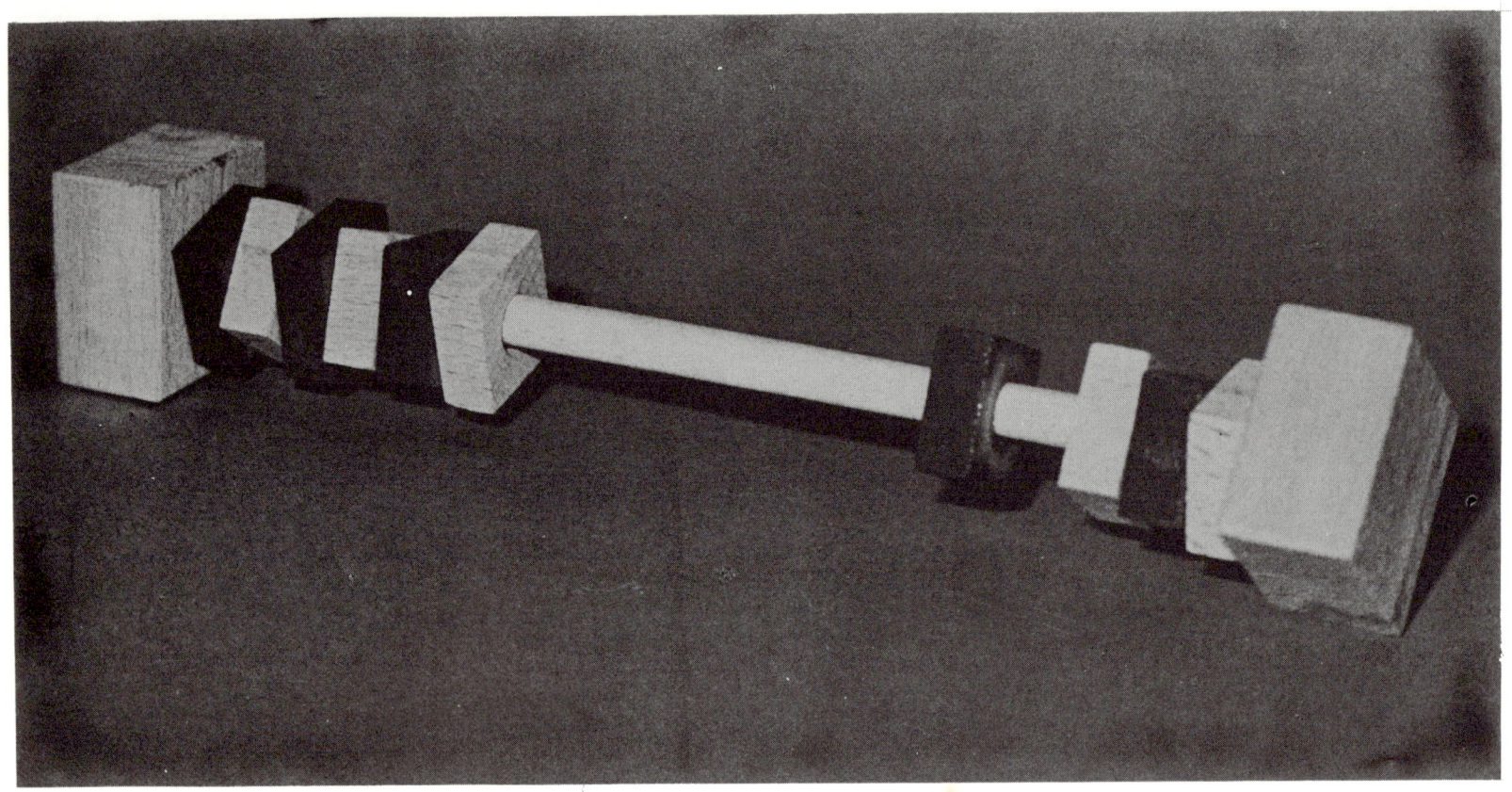

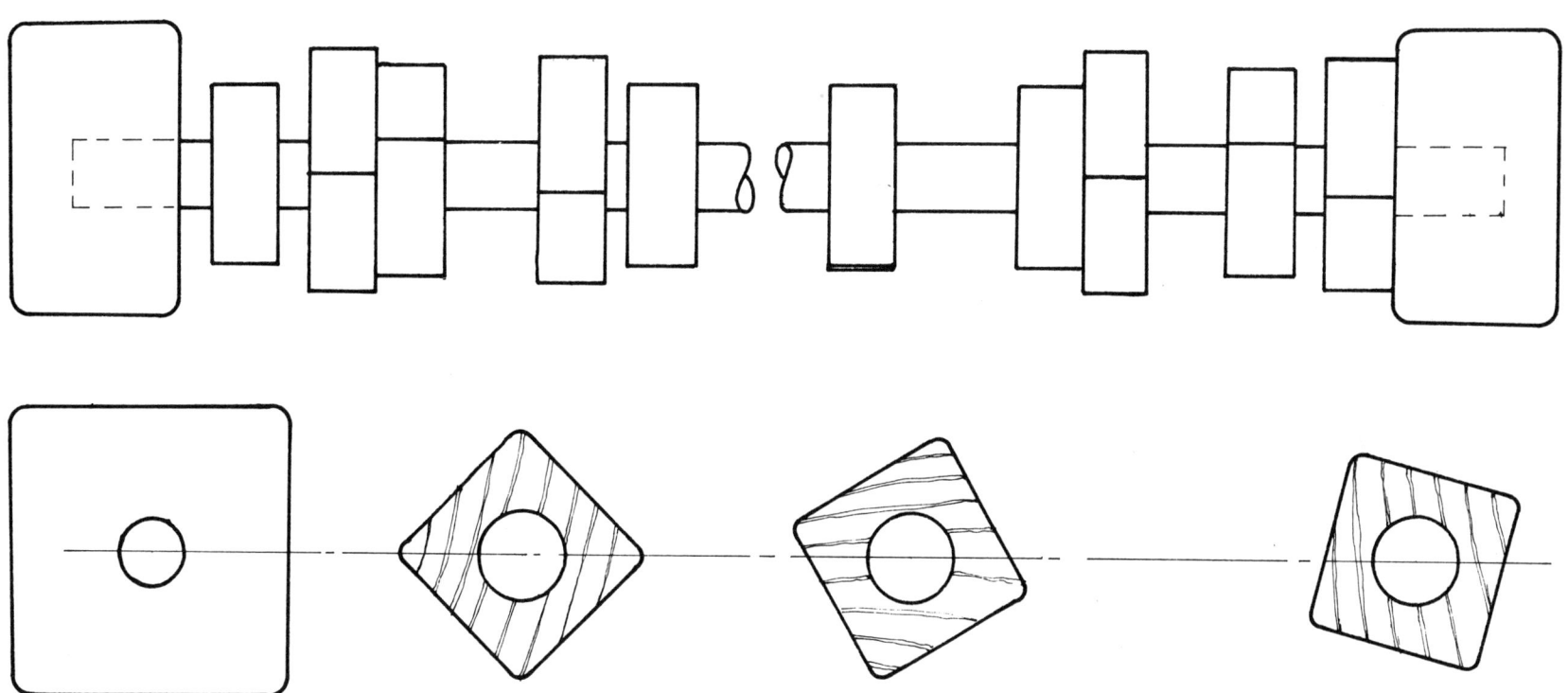

Counting Rod

Buttons, beads, marbles and beans for counting can easily get lost or misplaced. Here is a collection of ten sizable pieces of wood which can be moved along a 9" (230mm) length of $\frac{3}{8}$" (9mm) dowel; it will assist and amuse a child in the early stages of counting.

The toy is made from beech and the counters were drilled with end grain on, for ease of drilling. These are best held in a machine vice to prevent twisting. The end blocks are coloured, and the counters are painted in alternate colours to assist in the recognition of number. For painting, see page 96.

Jet Airliner

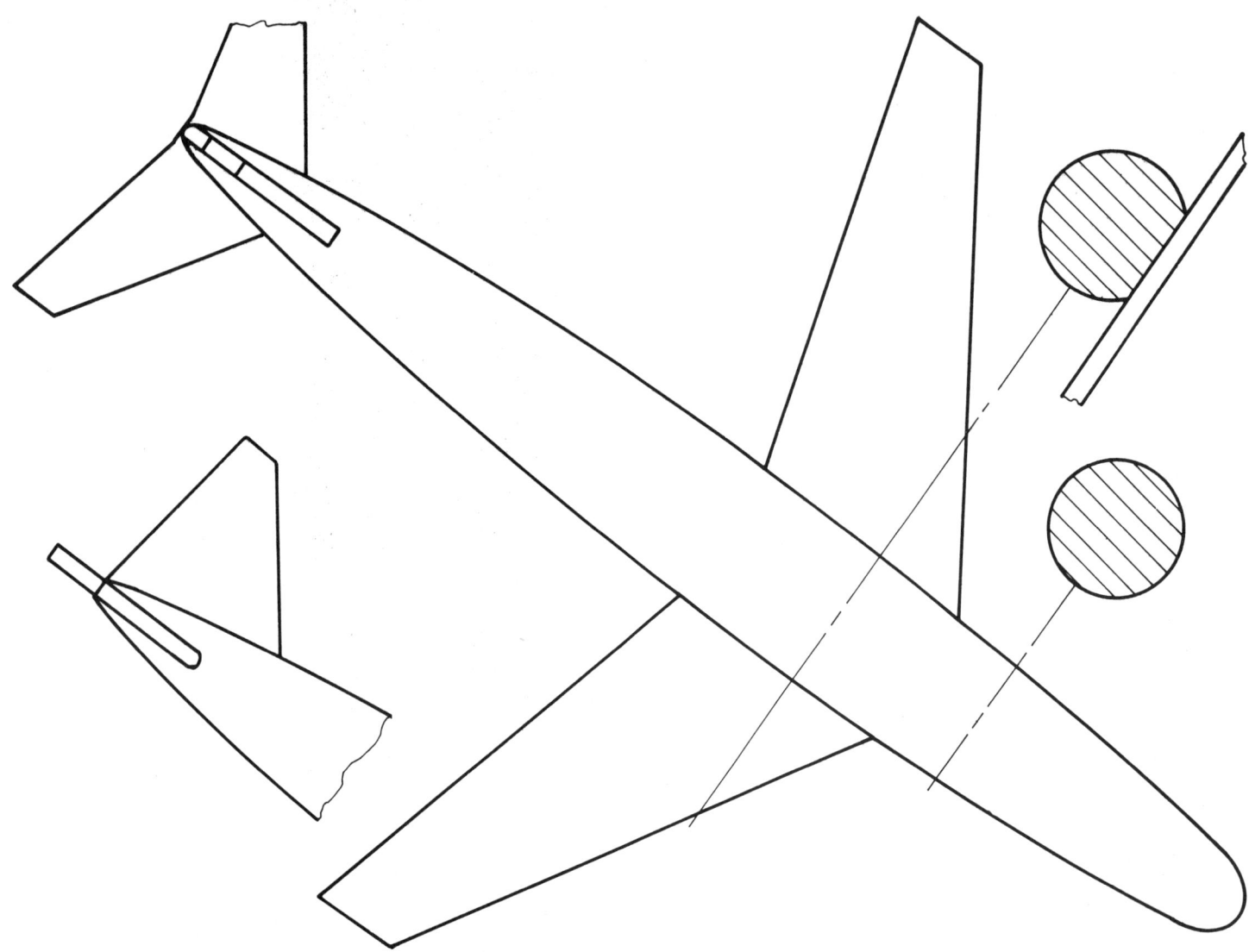

Jet Airliner

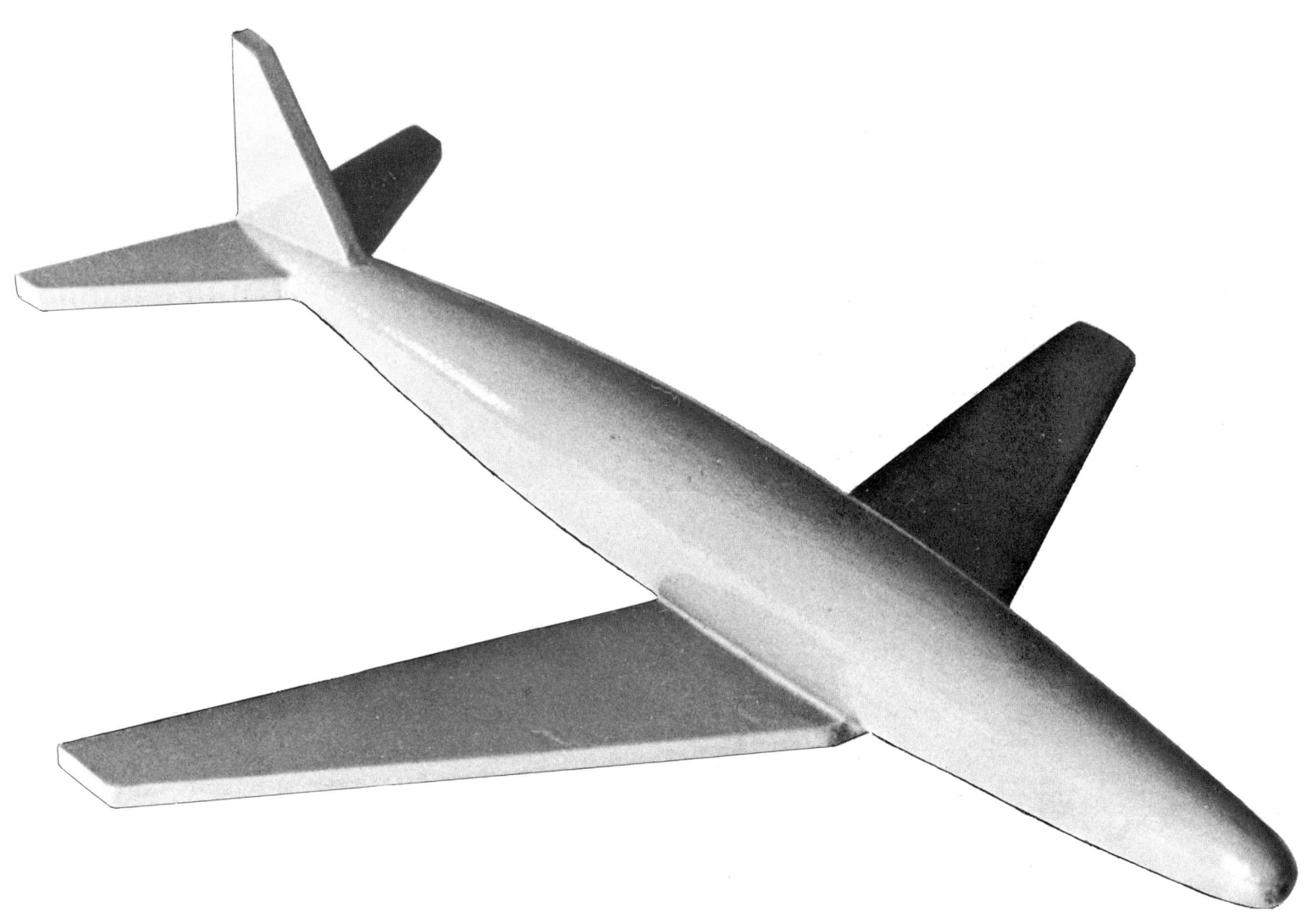

Jet Airliner

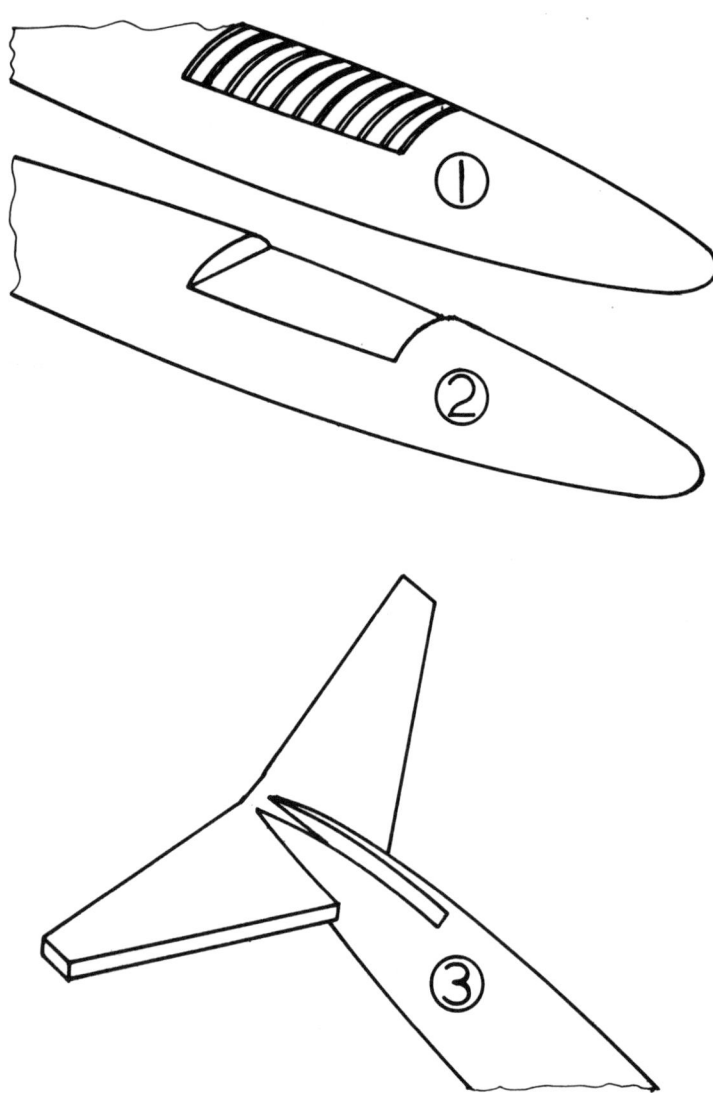

This is a toy to push along or whizz through the air, held in the hand. It could be suspended on a nylon thread as a junior bedroom item. The body was turned, but it could be shaped from a piece of broom handle; keep on a good length for holding in the hand or vice until the shaping is nearly complete. The wings and the rudder are marked out from paper templates (page 51) on to 3 or 4mm ply. The main wings, which are in one piece, are let into a shallow broad groove cut into the body. The tail, which is also made in one piece, is glued into a slot which is cut into the body. Two carefully made saw cuts would be necessary for the slot. When the tail glue is set then a groove can be nibbled out with a narrow chisel for the rudder. This toy had three coats of paint and was well cleaned down between coats with fine glasspaper. For painting, see page 96.

1 Saw cuts before chiselling out the groove for the wings
2 Completed groove
3 Slot in tail for rudder

Crane

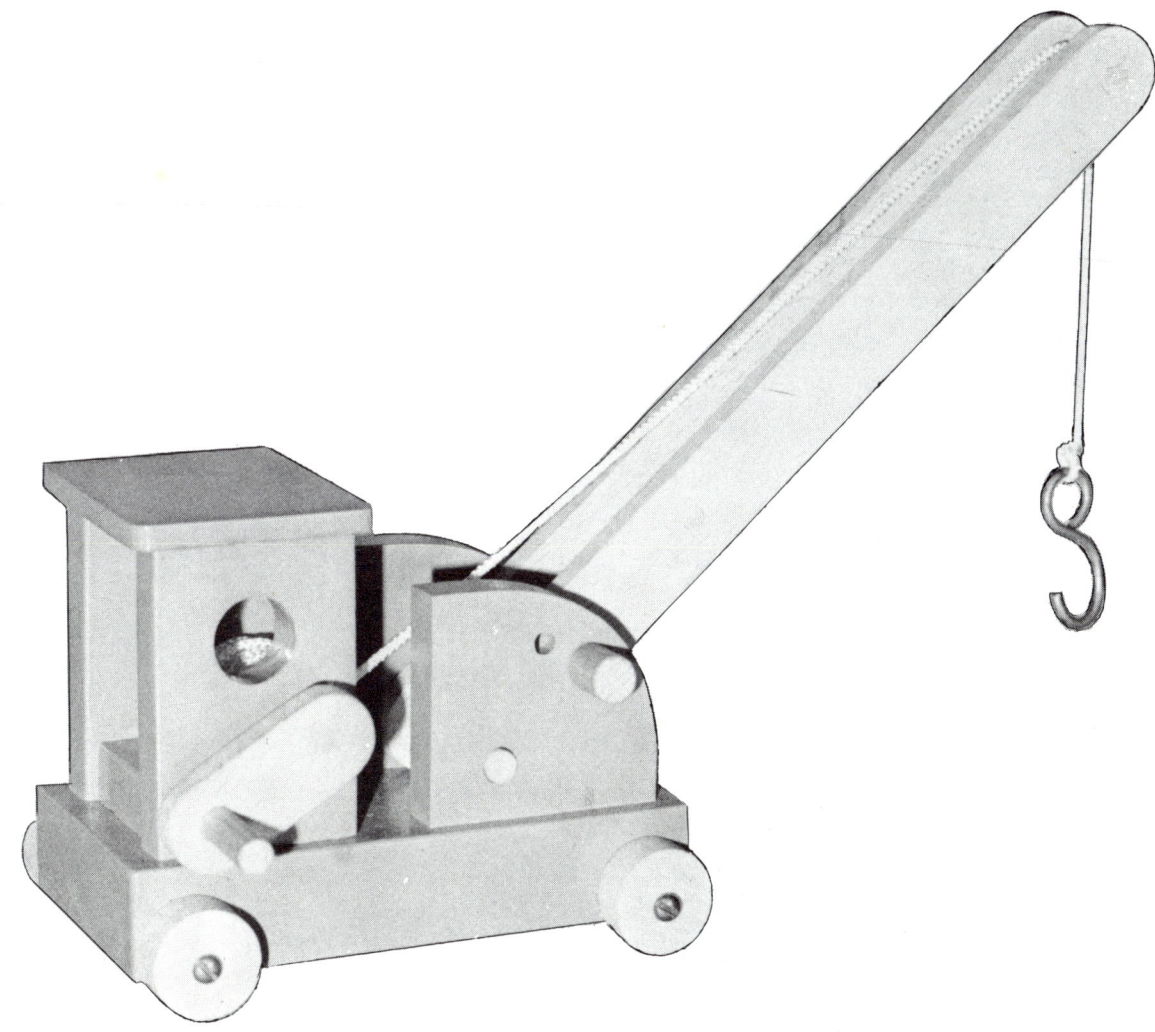

Crane

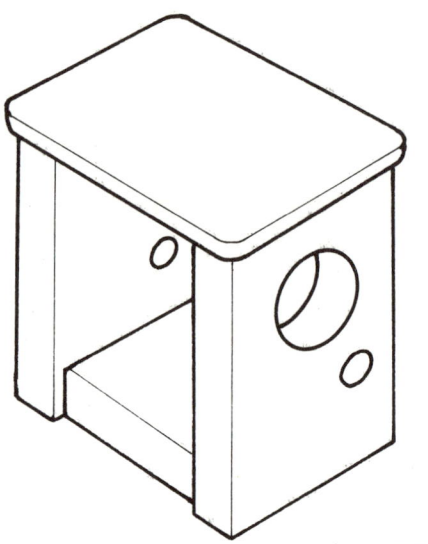

The important thing to remember when making this toy is that matching pieces must be drilled together, thus ensuring that all connecting or revolving dowels will line up easily. The winder and jib dowels are $\frac{3}{8}''$ (9mm). It is a good idea to place a piece of dowel in position before drilling the next hole, and so on. All dowels should be in position when gluing sides together, as this will ensure correct alignment. The winder shaft is kept in place with two pieces of $\frac{5}{8}''$ (15mm) dowel which have been drilled to fit. Squares of ply would do equally well. This is not one of the easier toys to make, but the construction involvement should satisfy a good craftsman. The toy is easier to make if the sides of the cabin and the jib base are made as one piece (page 66). All pieces are glued together with Resin W adhesive (PVA).

The wheels are cut from thick broom handle (page 94) or turned on a lathe. The toy can be painted, or lightly covered with a clear varnish, or left plain.

Crane

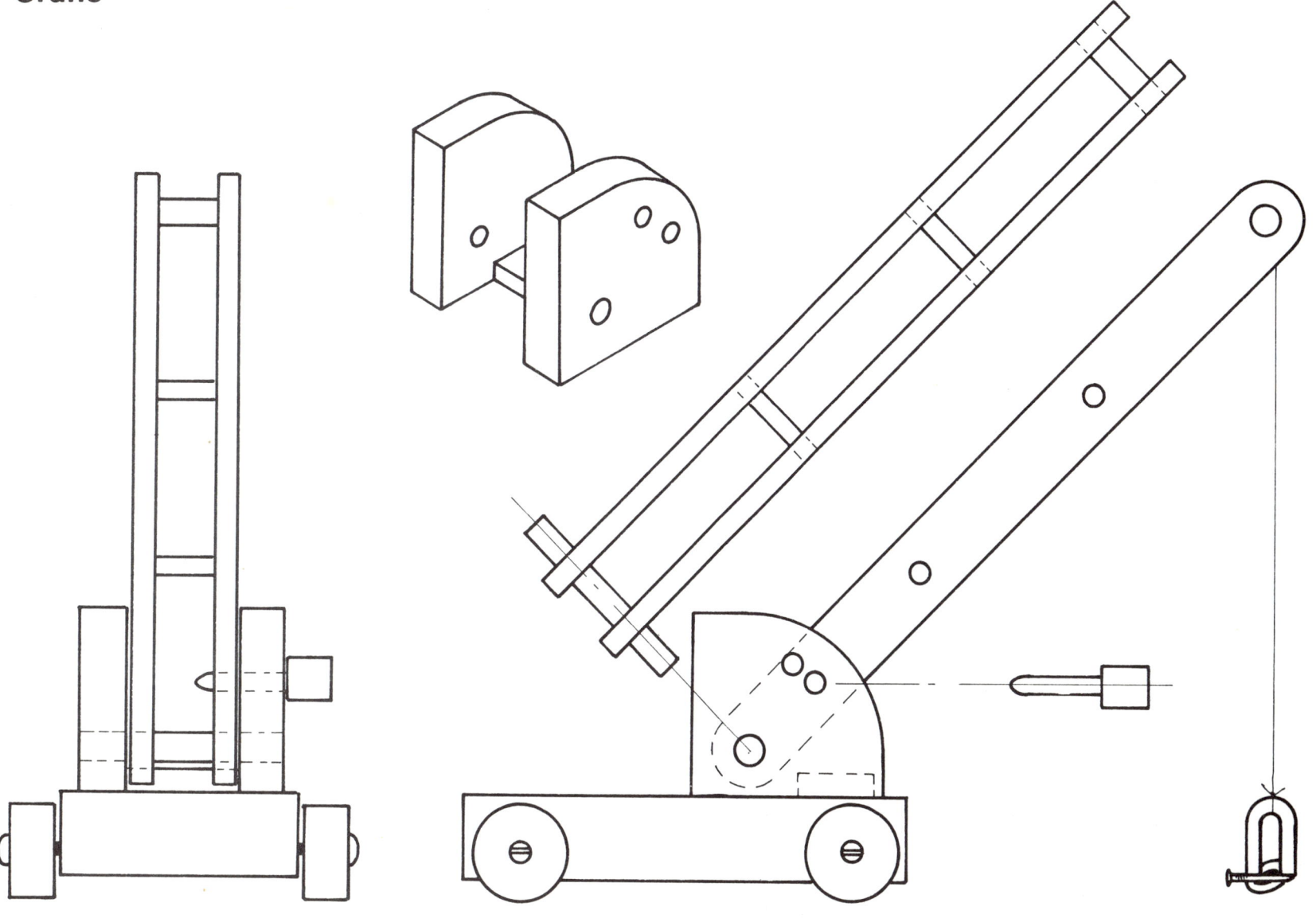

Crane

The side of the cabin and the side of the crane can be
made in one piece.

Rotating Crane

This crane rotates on a base to which it is located by a $\frac{1}{4}''$ (6mm) coach bolt. The bolt can be locked by tightening a second nut against the first. A plywood spacer is well waxed (candle) and is set between the base and the revolving head.

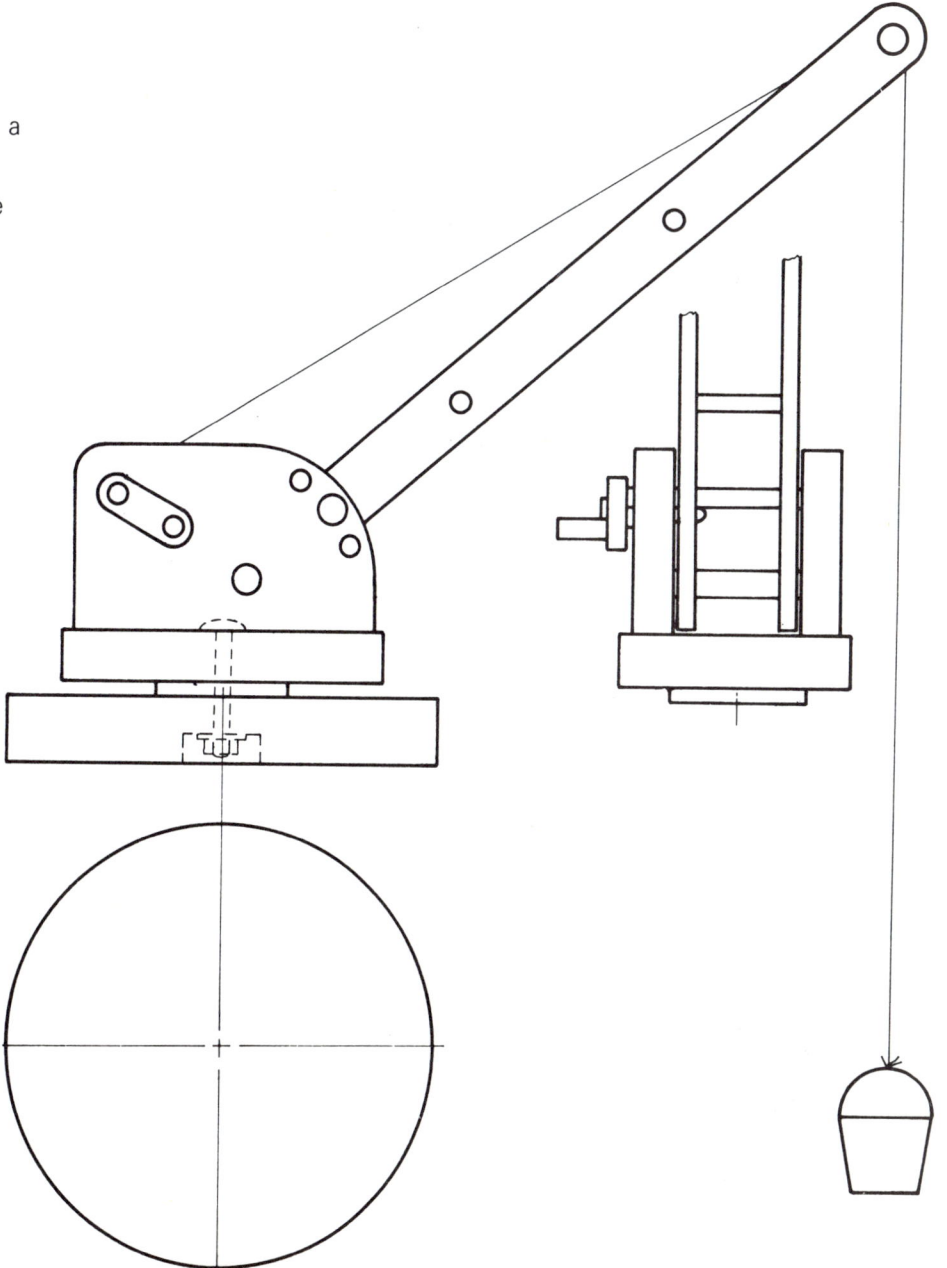

Concorde

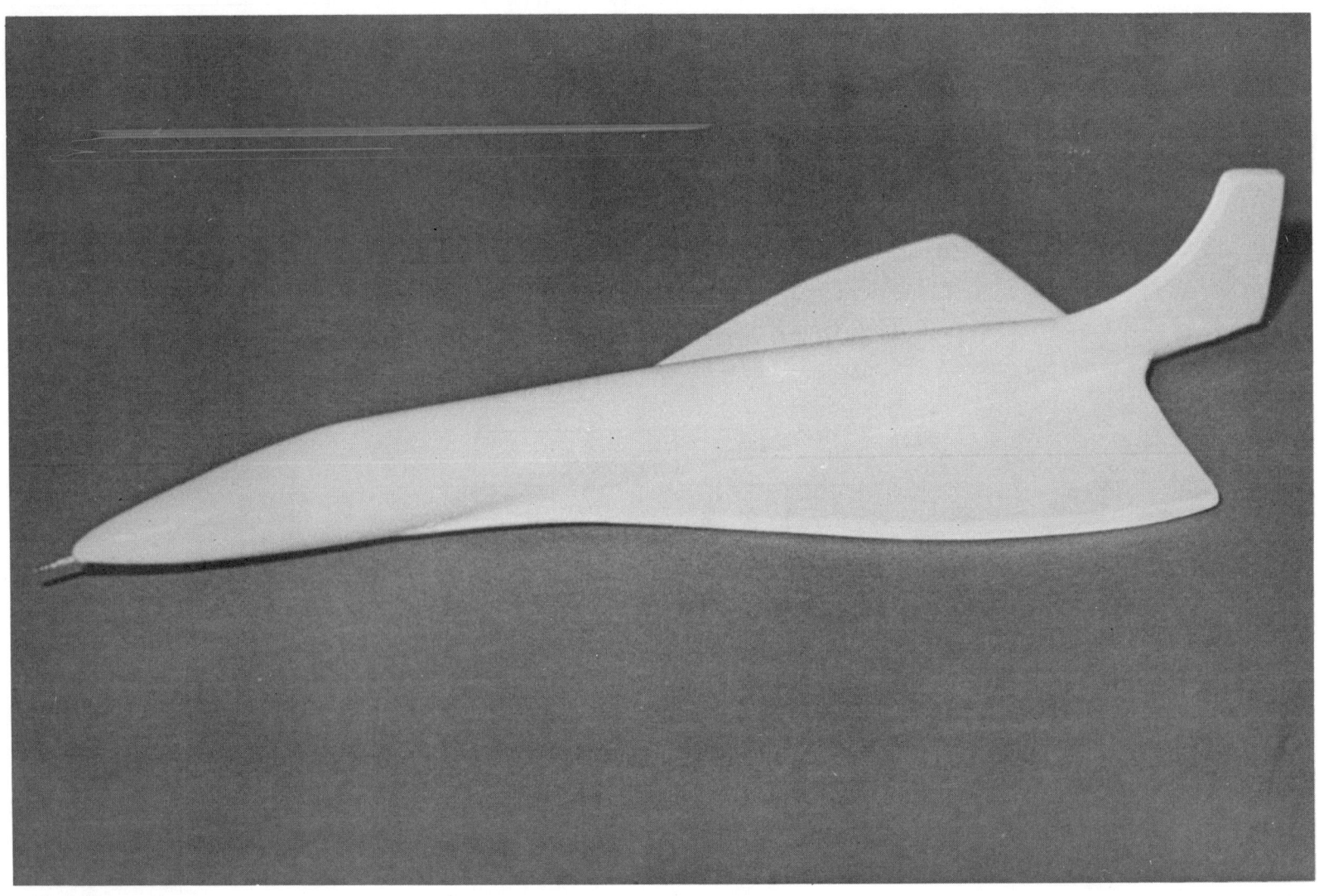

Concorde

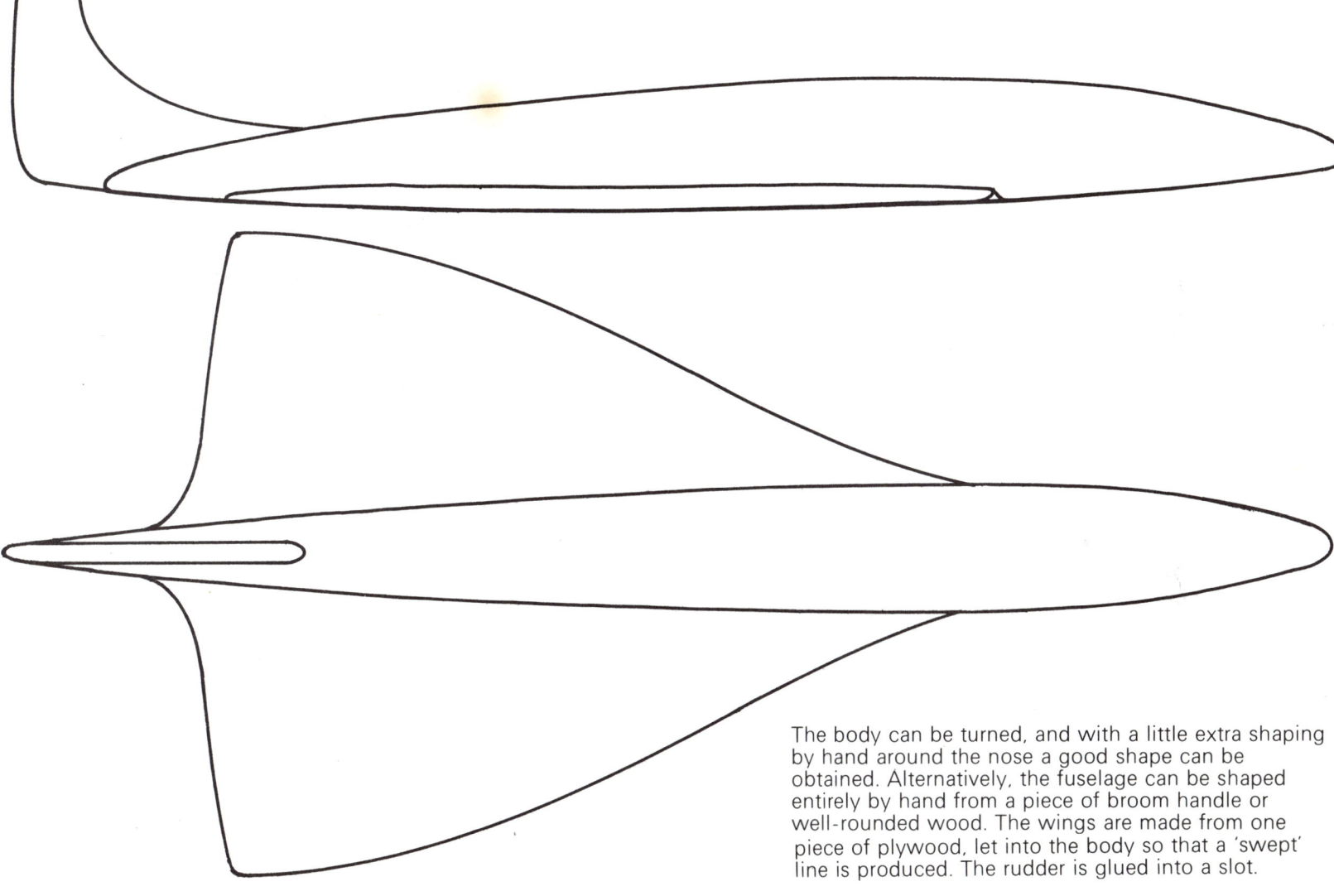

The body can be turned, and with a little extra shaping by hand around the nose a good shape can be obtained. Alternatively, the fuselage can be shaped entirely by hand from a piece of broom handle or well-rounded wood. The wings are made from one piece of plywood, let into the body so that a 'swept' line is produced. The rudder is glued into a slot.

Chunky Animals

Chunky Animals

These are made from odd pieces of 1¼″ and 1½″ (30 and 40mm) thick materials, and could be used as pieces of sculpture when the play requirement has diminished. Any sound pieces of wood could be used, although the grain run should be considered for the duck's beak, otherwise it may break across the short grain. Holes drilled on both sides of the duck's neck will simplify the cutting of the outline. The elephant's trunk is separated from the body by a 1″ (25mm) hole. The animals can be painted, varnished, or left as plain wood. For painting, see page 96.

Chunky Animals

Chunky Animals

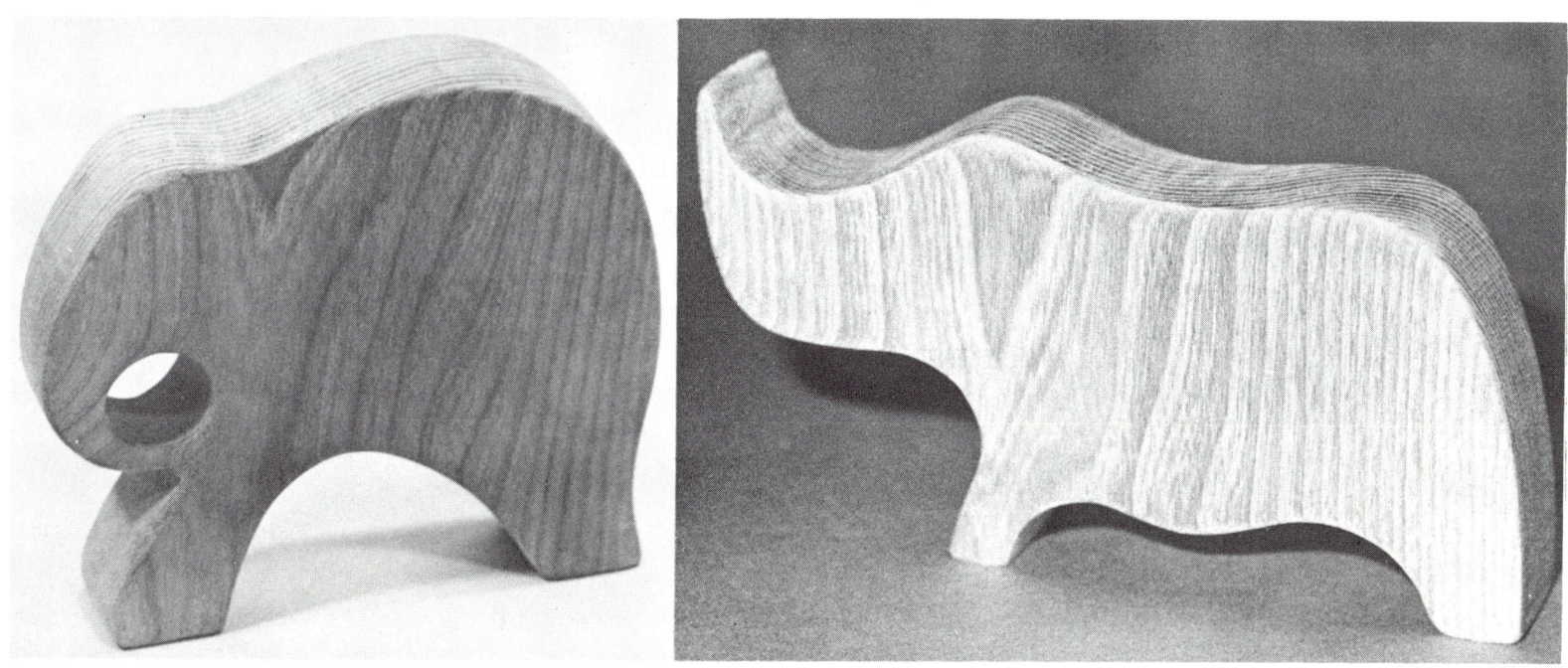

Yo-yo 1

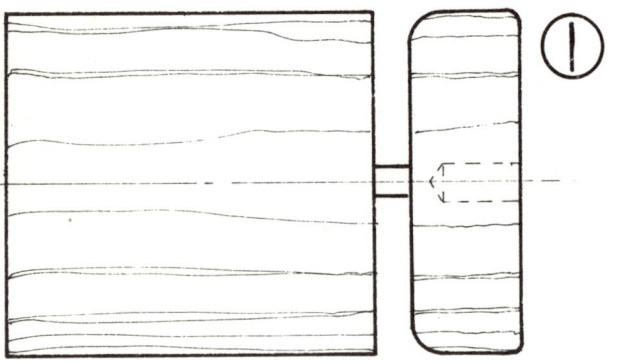

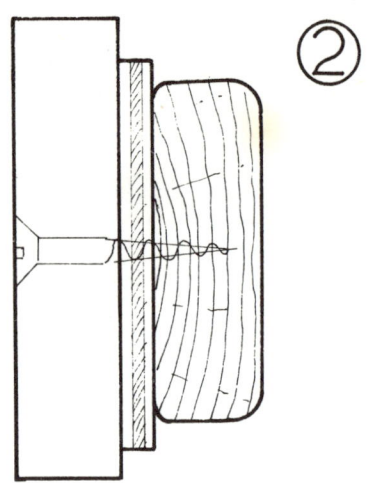

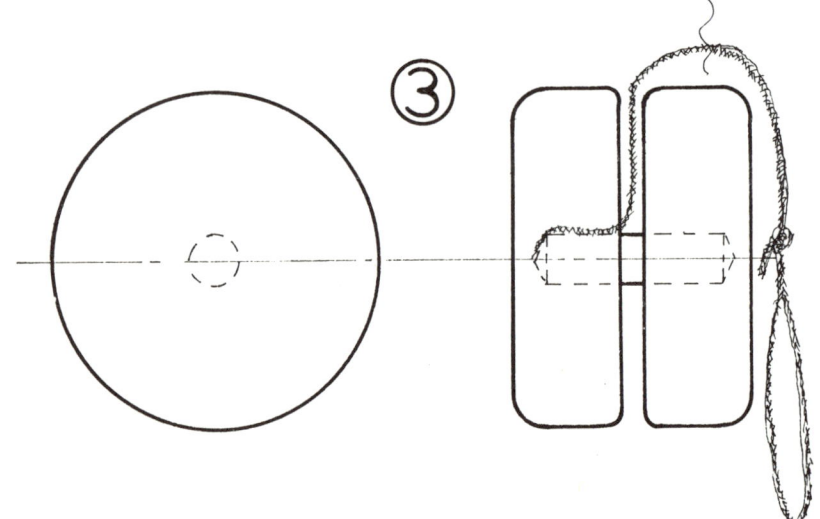

This yo-yo is turned on a lathe.

1   Turning in a ring chuck with tail stock support. $\frac{5}{8}'' \times 1\frac{3}{4}''$ (15 × 45mm).

2   Turning on a single screw face plate with a plywood backing-piece to prevent the turning tool from touching the metal. The wood is prepared to $\frac{5}{8}''$ thickness and cut roughly to shape for turning.

3   The two halves are turned and glued together with a $\frac{1}{4}''$ (6mm) dowel. Use 2mm spacing strips to ensure an even gap. At the time of gluing a 3′ (1m) length of very thin twine or nylon string should be anchored in a hole.

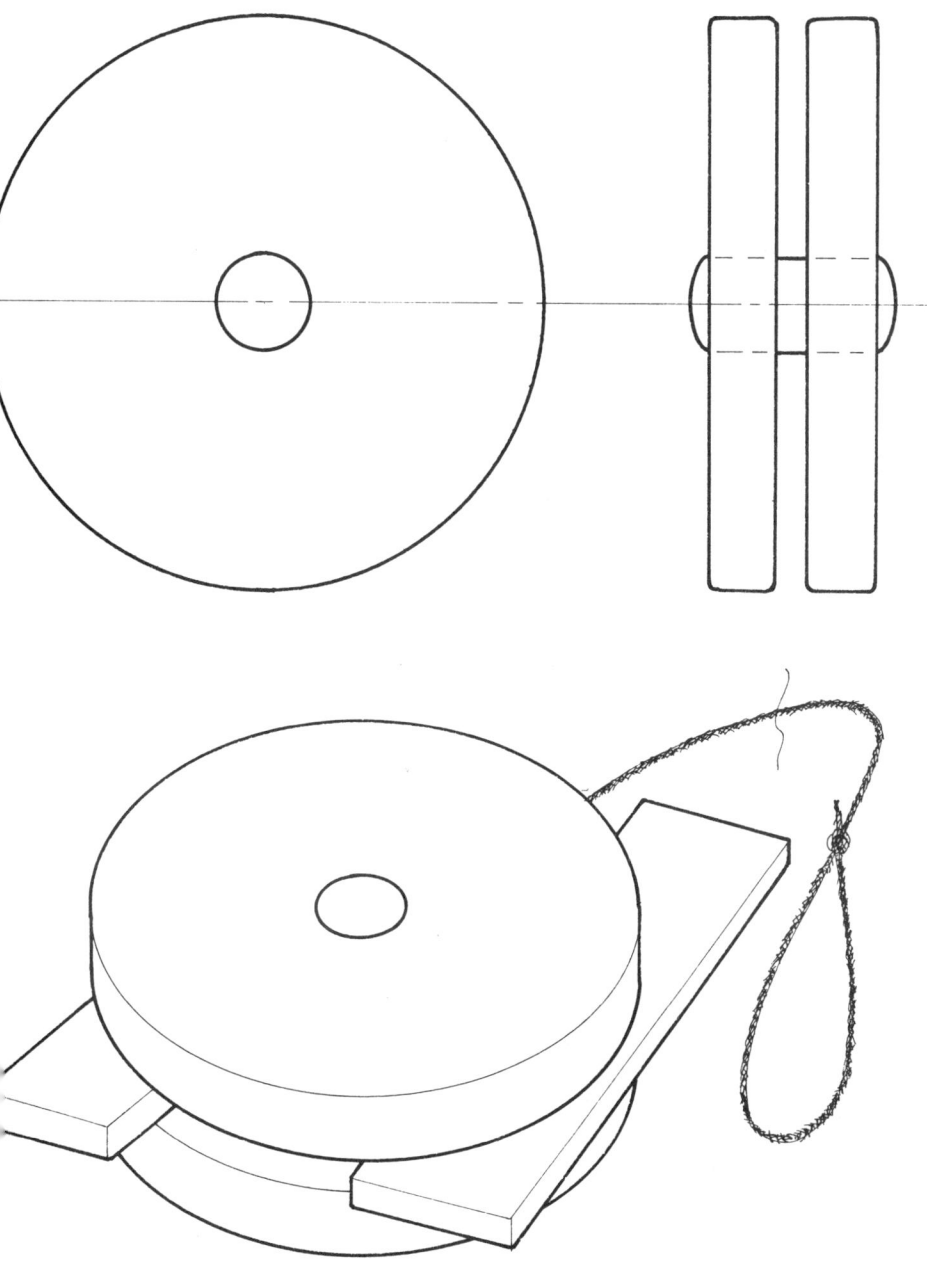

Yo-yo 2

Here is a yo-yo shaped by hand. The plates can be made from $\frac{3}{8}''$ (9mm) flat well-seasoned wood or plywood. They can be cut to a circular shape with a coping saw, or the corners can be cut off with a tenon saw and finally pared to shape with a sharp chisel against a smooth piece of wood. The $\frac{1}{2}''$ dowel can be stopped, made flush or rounded to stand slightly clear of the surfaces of the plates.

Gluing the string and dowel to the plates. The 4mm strips will assist in even spacing.

Rocking Horse

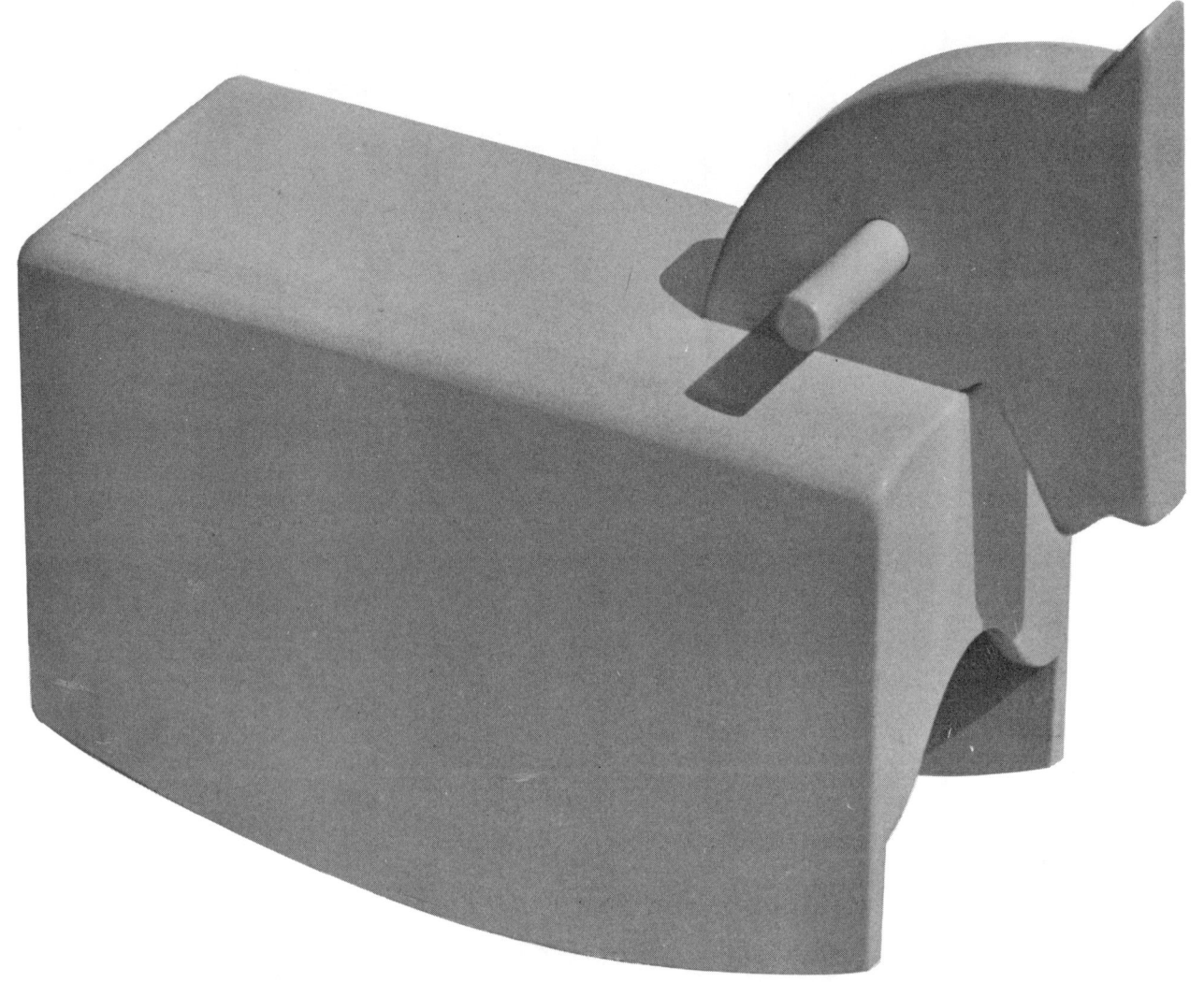

Rocking Horse

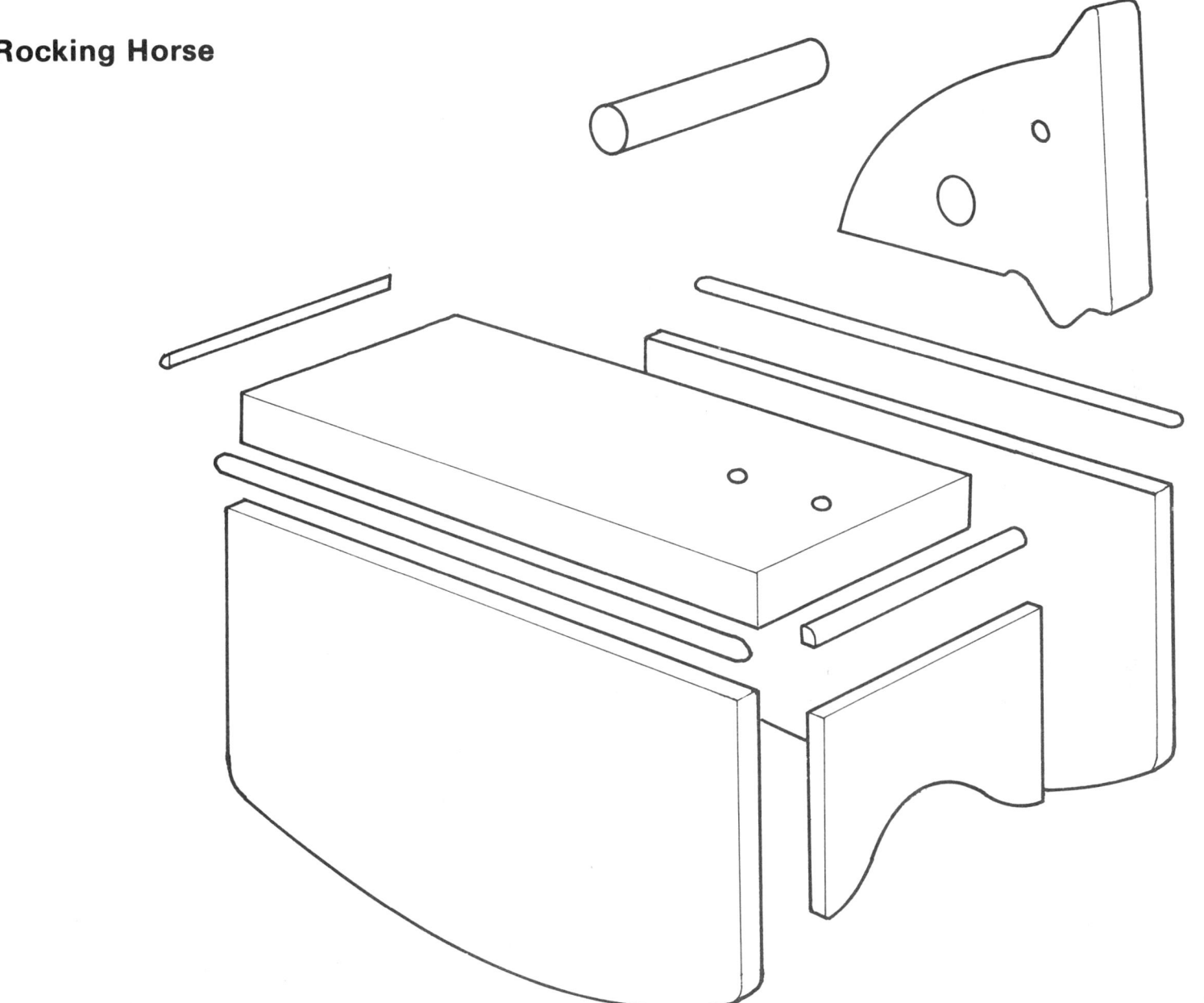

Rocking Horse

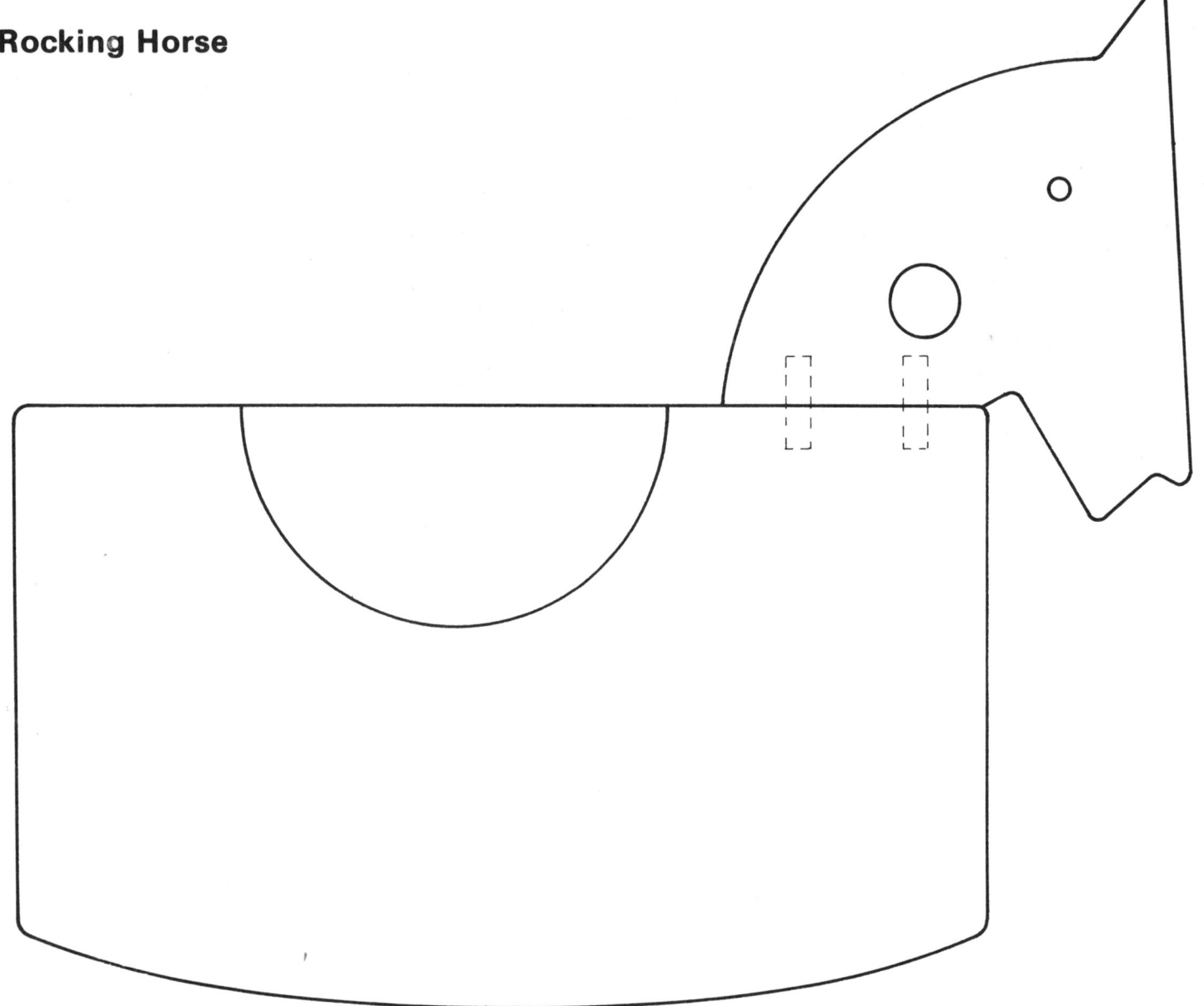

Rocking Horse

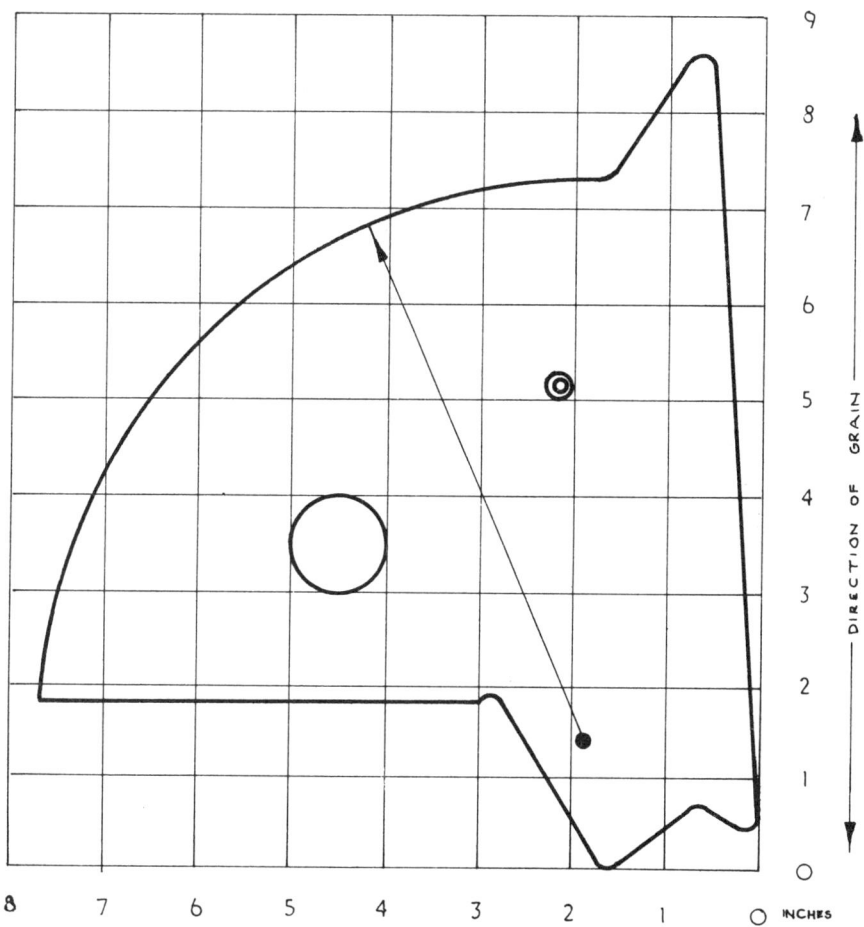

9
8
7
6
5
4

DIRECTION OF GRAIN

3
2
1
0

8 7 6 5 4 3 2 1 0 INCHES

This is a sturdy toy which a child will love to have. It will serve as a seat as well as a rocker. The seat is made from a piece of wood 6″ × 14″ × 1¼″ (150 × 355 × 30mm). The sides, which are made from ½″ (12mm) blockboard, can have the edges lipped with solid wood (glued and nailed) or just filled with a wood filler to make reasonable surfaces for painting. The sides are glued and nailed on to the seat. The front and back panels are similar and are shaped, glued and nailed on to the seat. The rounded seat edges can be glued on afterwards or glued on to the panels as lipping. The head is cut from 1¼″ (30mm) material and can be drawn on a grid of 1″ (25mm) squares. The handle can be specially turned on a lathe to fit a 1″ hole, or a piece of broom handle can be used. The head is located on the body with two ⅜″ (9mm) dowels before being glued. After thoroughly cleaning and smoothing with glasspaper the rocker can be painted. The choice is wide and is yours. Advice on paints is given on page 96.

Rocking Horse

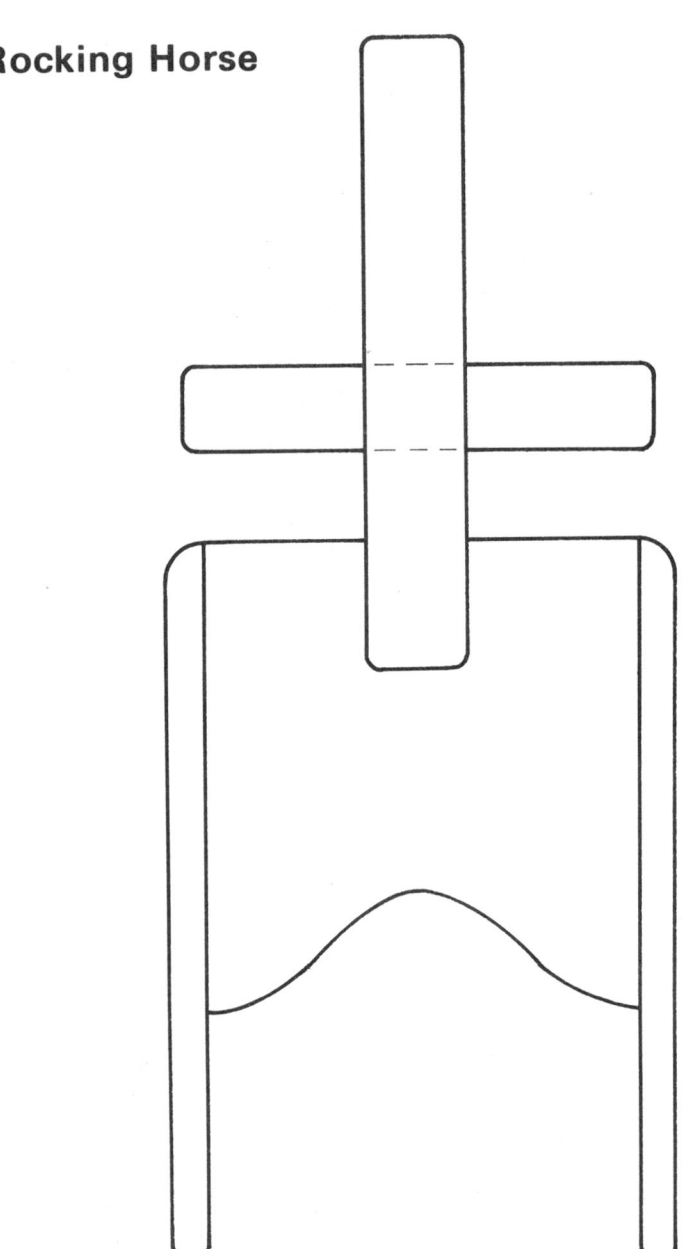

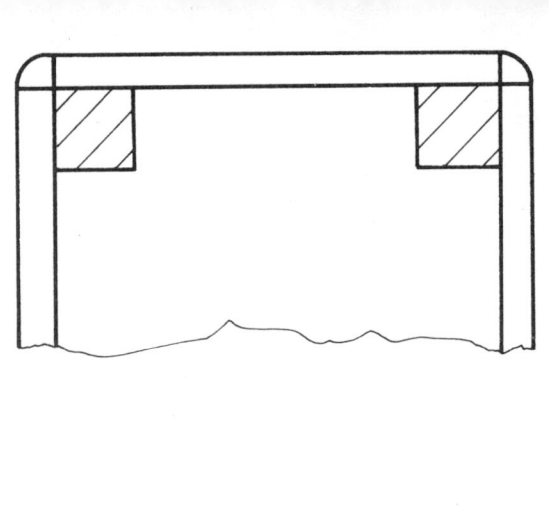

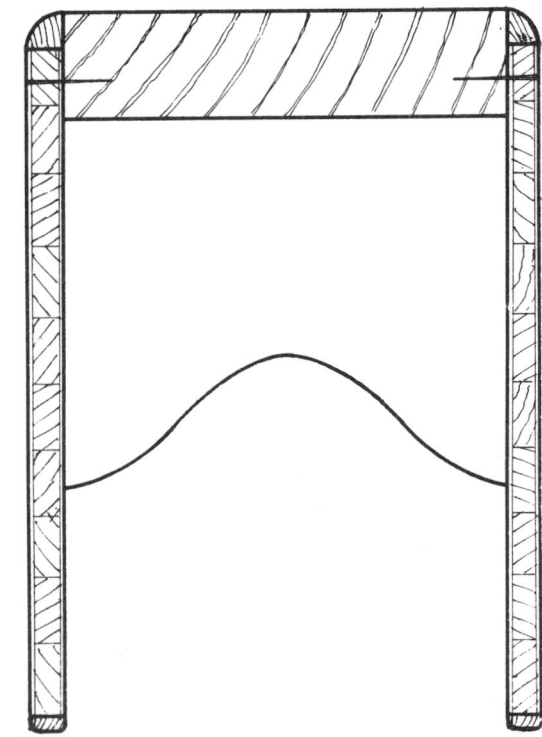

Rocking Duck

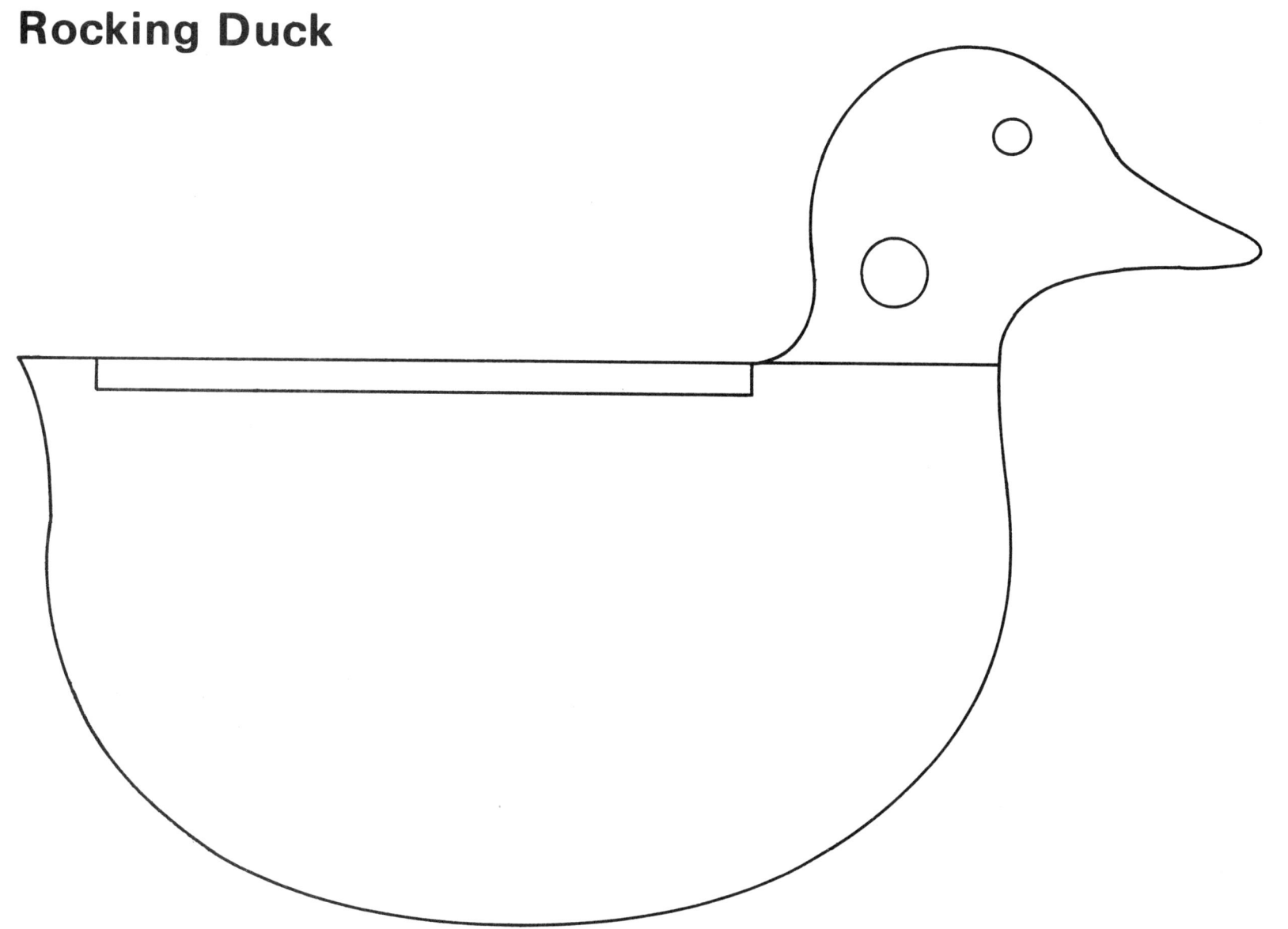

Rocking Duck

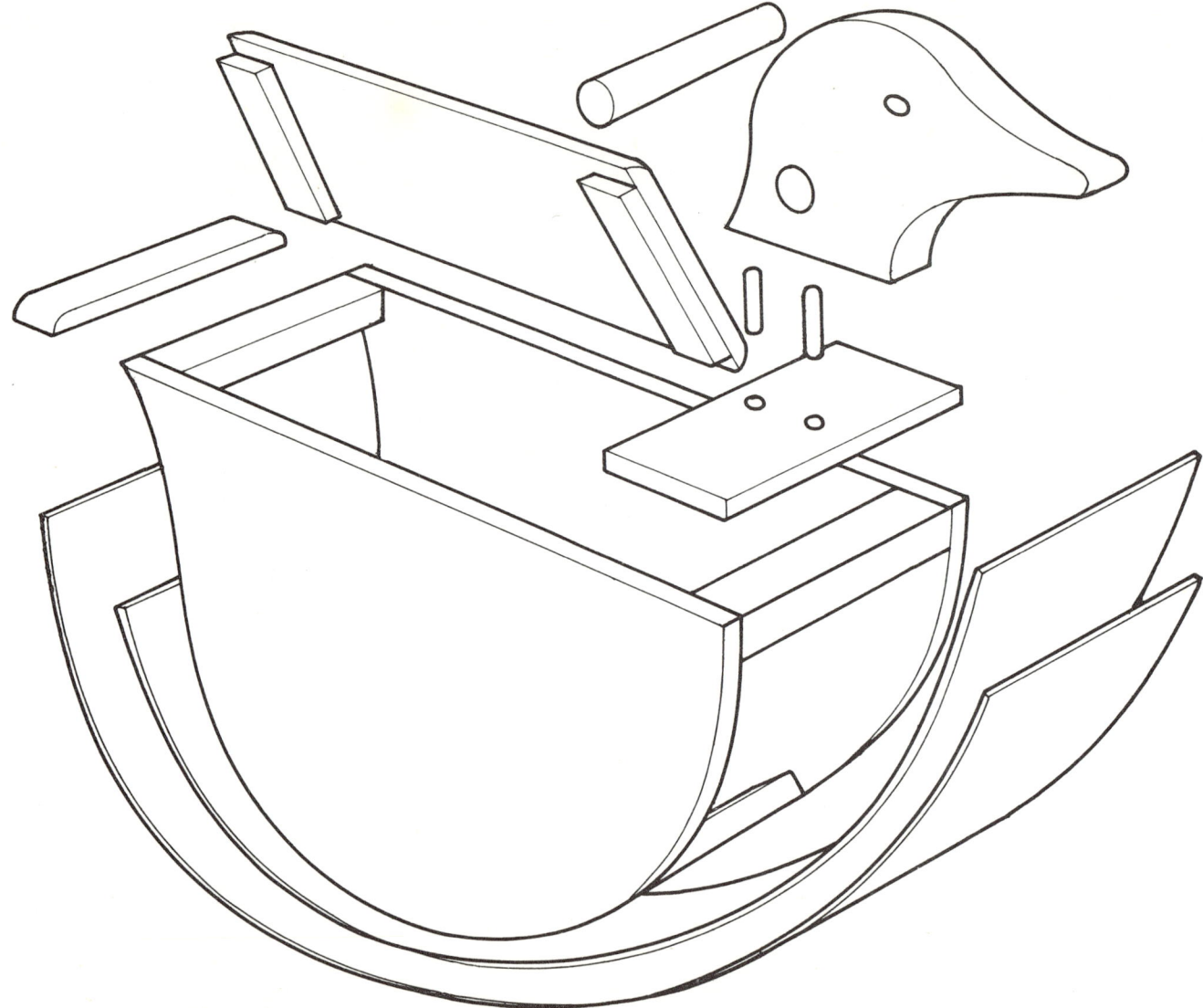

Rocking Duck

This is an interesting variation on the rocking horse. It can be made as a full rocker and used for toy storage. The two side panels of $\frac{1}{2}$" (12mm) were cut from pieces measuring 17"×9" (430×230mm); $\frac{3}{8}$" (9mm) plywood can also be used. The four cross rails are 6" (150mm) long and are cut from $1\frac{1}{2}$" square and $1\frac{1}{2}$"×1" (40×25mm) material. The side panels are glued and nailed to the rails. Two 7" (180mm) strips of 3 or 4mm ply are cut for the rocking surface. These should be cut with the surface grain running across, to make them easy to flex. When the glue on the body assembly is set, then the ply strips can be glued and nailed around. The double thickness of ply will make the rocking surface very strong. The removable seat and the tail and head boards are cut from $\frac{1}{4}$" (12mm) blockboard or $\frac{3}{8}$" ply and are glued and nailed in place.

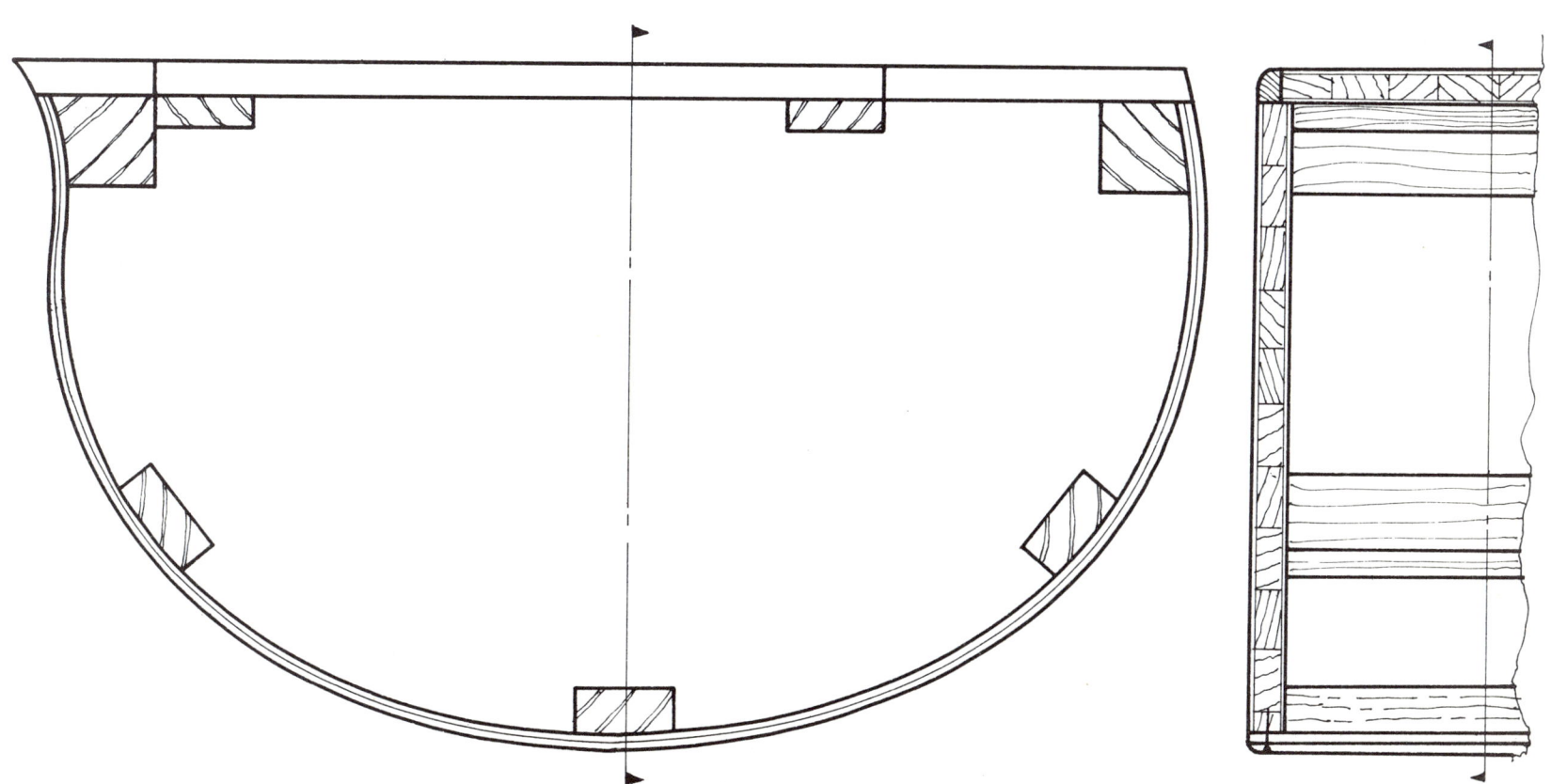

Rocking Duck

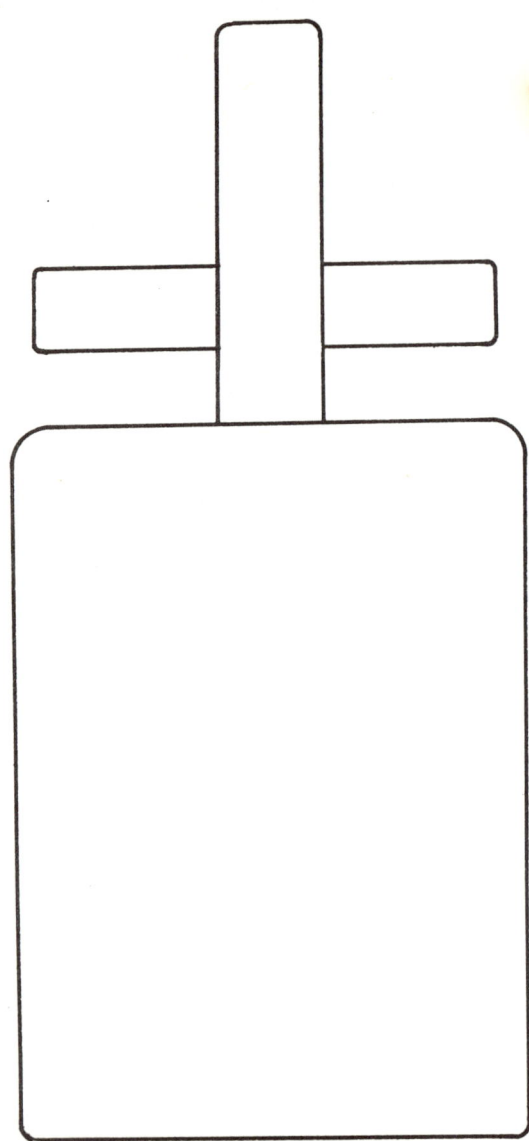

The duck's head is cut from $1\frac{1}{4}''$ (30mm) wood, and the grain run should be noted to prevent splitting across the beak. The handle can be turned or cut from a piece of broom handle, and glued into a hole drilled in the head. There is enough surface gluing area on the head for it to be glued straight on to the head board, but dowels can be used if preferred. The whole toy should be thoroughly cleaned and smoothed before being painted. The head could be painted in contrast to the body and seat. For painting, see page 96.

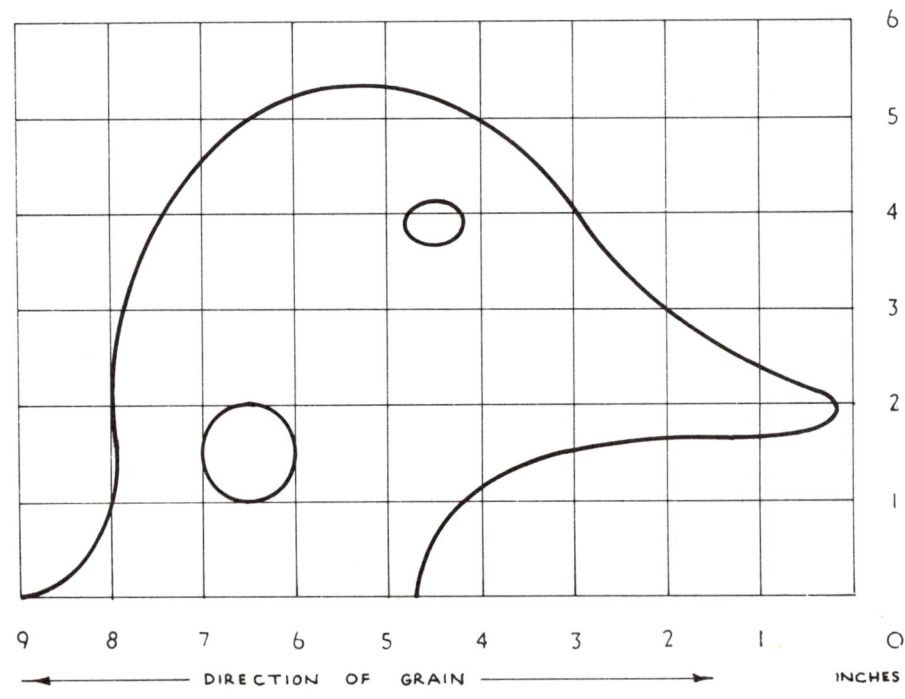

9 8 7 6 5 4 3 2 1 0

←——— DIRECTION OF GRAIN ———→ INCHES

Biplane

Biplane

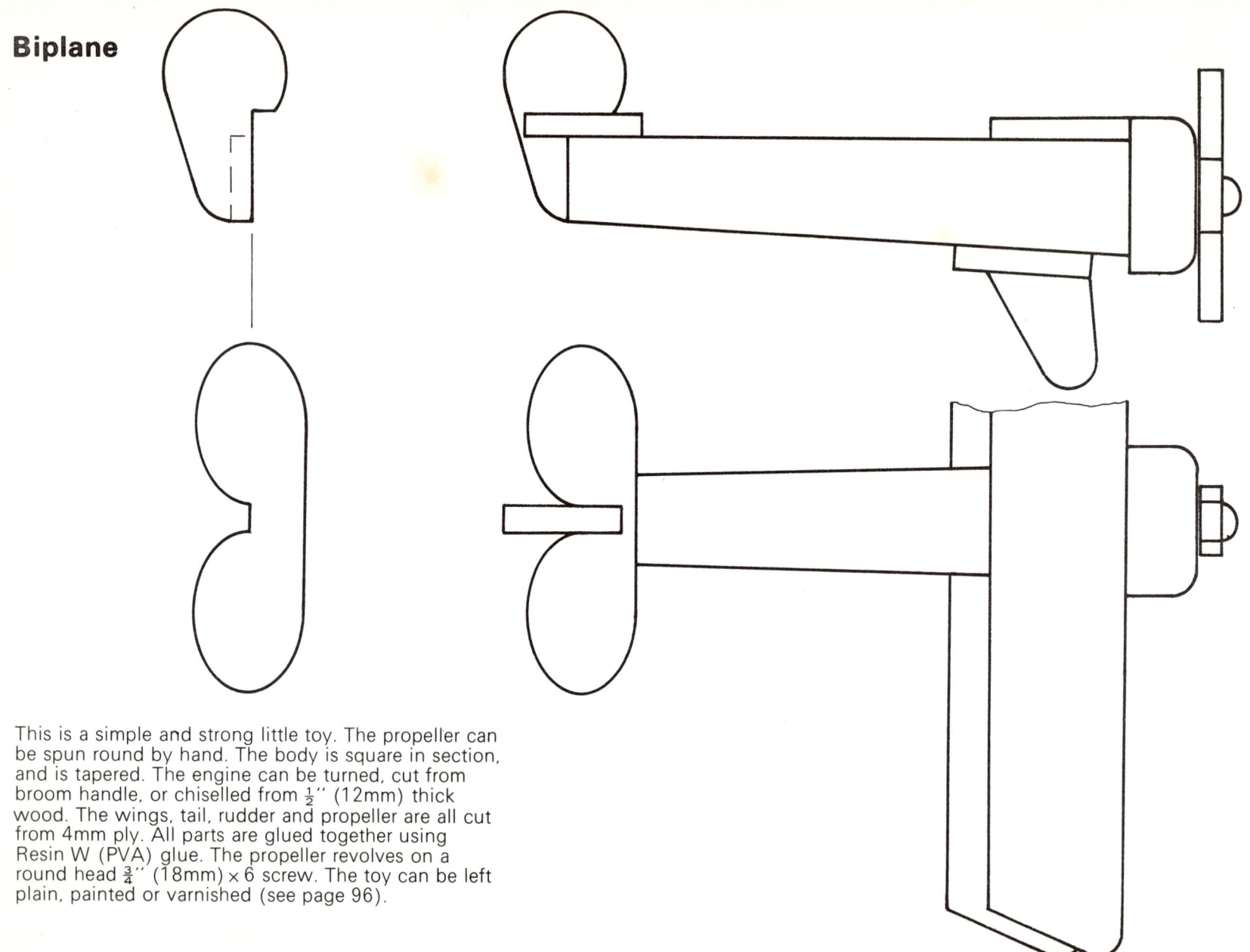

This is a simple and strong little toy. The propeller can be spun round by hand. The body is square in section, and is tapered. The engine can be turned, cut from broom handle, or chiselled from $\frac{1}{2}''$ (12mm) thick wood. The wings, tail, rudder and propeller are all cut from 4mm ply. All parts are glued together using Resin W (PVA) glue. The propeller revolves on a round head $\frac{3}{4}''$ (18mm) × 6 screw. The toy can be left plain, painted or varnished (see page 96).

Biplane

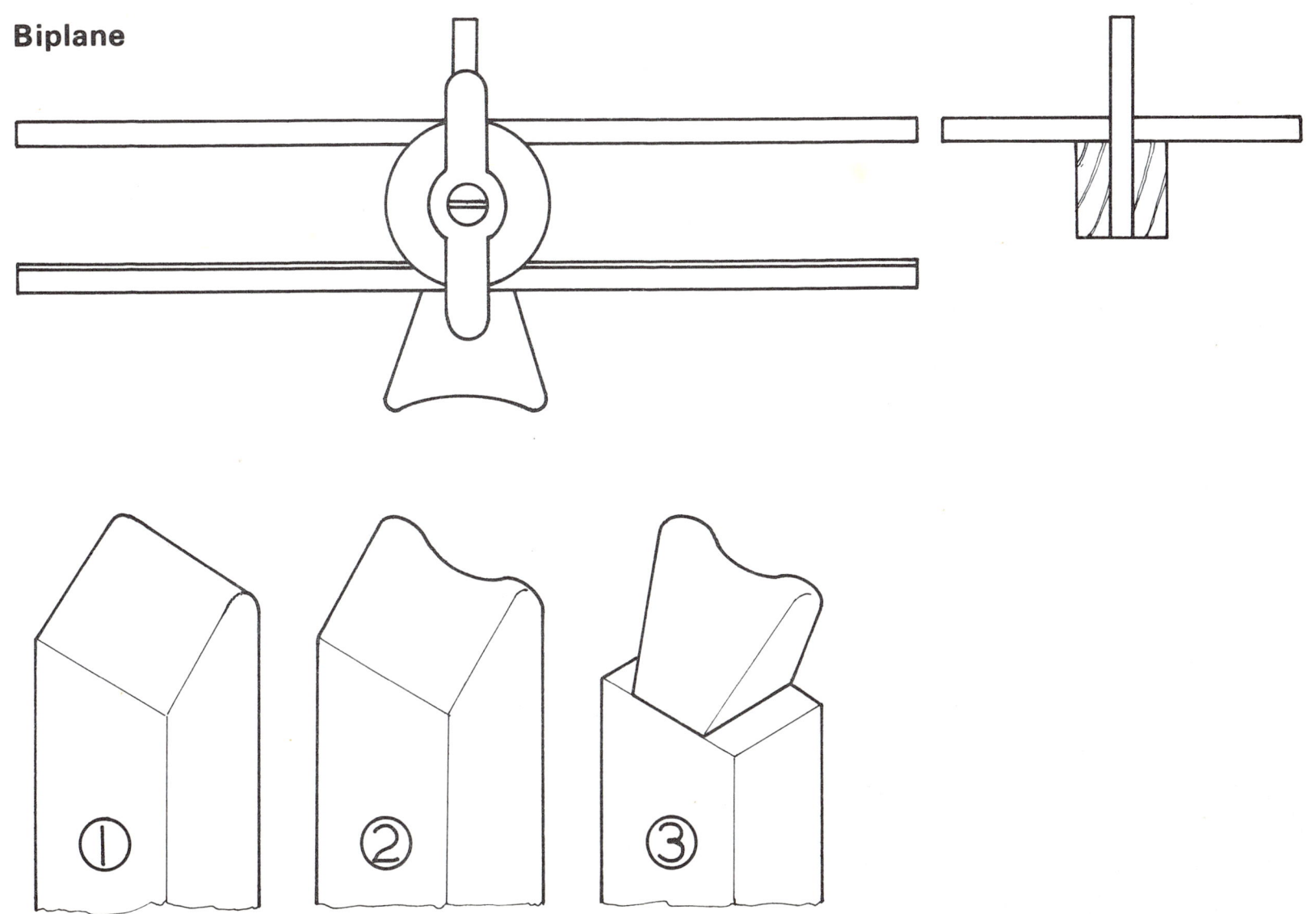

Stages in cutting the undercarriage

Information Box

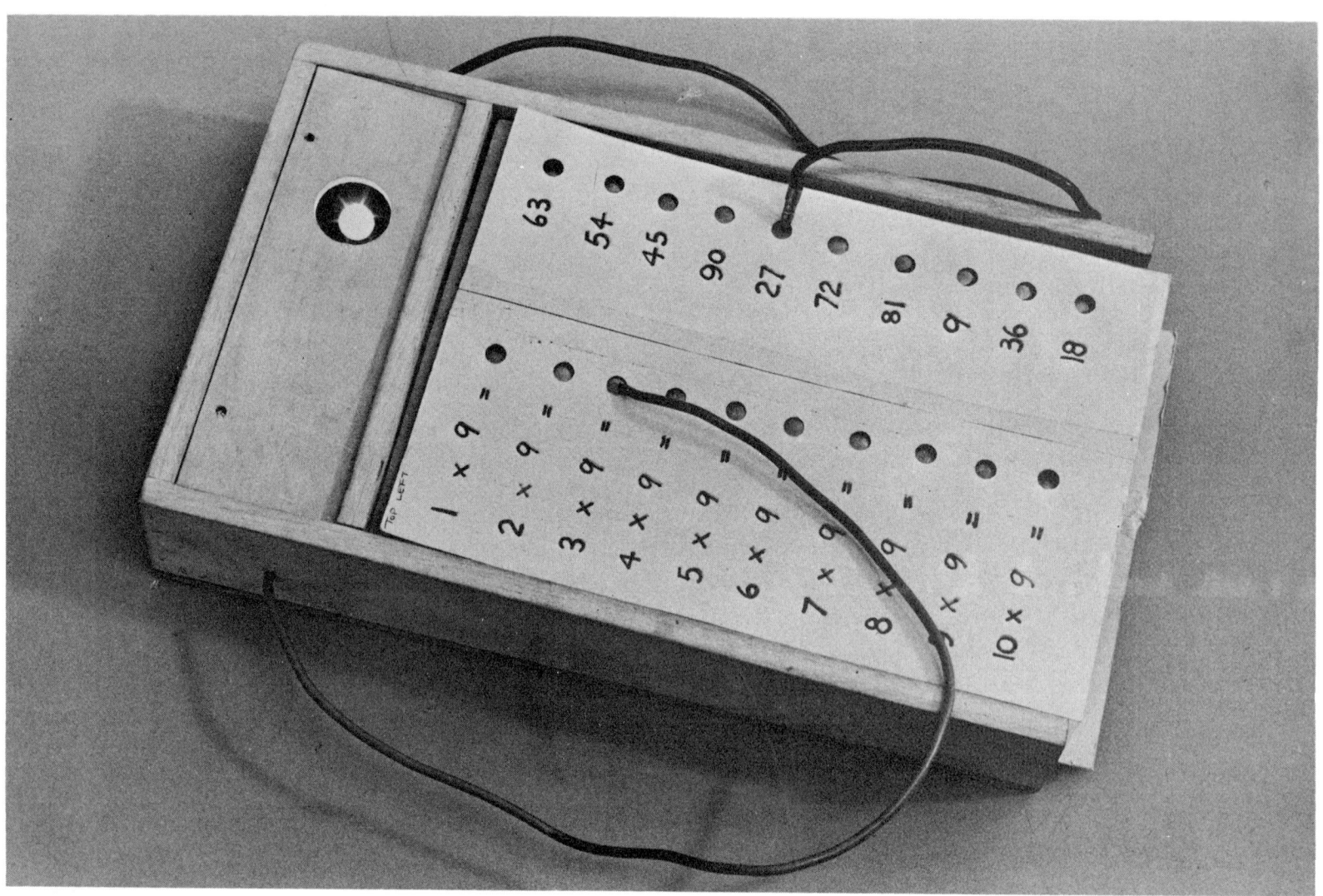

Information Box

This is an amusing and instructive toy. To get a response through a light when one selects a correct answer to a question is not new. Even when a set of questions and answers is programmed in a box with a torch battery and bulb, that is not new either; but there are a number of ideas in this particular model which are new.

The box measures $11'' \times 7'' \times 2''$ ($280 \times 180 \times 50$mm) and the sides, end and partition are $\frac{3}{8}''$ (9mm) thick. These are glued and lightly pinned together on to a plywood base. The electrical wiring for the question and answer panel is set between two sheets of plywood which are $8\frac{1}{2}''$ (240mm) long and sufficiently wide to fit inside the box. The two layers enclose the wiring and protect it, and prevent cheating to see where the wires go. These pieces of plywood are spaced apart at the ends with two strips of $\frac{3}{8}''$ (9mm) square material, which are glued to the top piece of ply and screwed to the lower. This panel slides on two $\frac{3}{8}''$ square strips of wood which are glued and pinned to the inside of the box. A torch bulb holder and small round battery are secured in the top compartment and two wandering leads are attached; the circuit can be tested by bringing the ends together to see if the bulb will light up. This compartment is covered with a panel of ply except for a $\frac{3}{4}''$ (18mm) diameter light hole. It can be a wedge fit or screwed down.

Now the aim is to get the bulb to light up through a circuit in the panel. Two methods for making contact on the panel are available. One uses brass paper fasteners to which thin wire is soldered; and the other method employs brass drawing pins, when no soldering will be required. Whichever method is selected the aim is the same: to pass a wire from a drawing pin in the question column to one in the answer column and thus make a complete circuit through to the bulb.

If paper fasteners are used they are pressed into a hole through the ply and the legs spread on the underside. Thin cotton-covered wire is ideal for soldering to the legs. If uncovered wire is used then it must be covered with gummed strip paper before the next wire is laid, to prevent a mix-up of circuits.

If drawing pins are used as contacts, they can be pressed through the ply and then withdrawn. The thin wire is then passed through the hole, the drawing pin replaced and the wire twisted round the shank of the pin before the excess wire is broken off. This is now repeated with a drawing pin in the other column.

The question and answer cards are now prepared to the size of the panel, and holes are punched through with a paper punch so that the drawing pins can be seen through the holes. If the paper punch used has a short throat then the holes can be made on the edges of the card for both questions and answers and of course the contact points (drawing pins or paper fasteners) must also be in line. This is the arrangement shown in the sketch on page 92. The questions are limitless and cards can be prepared on all topics: general knowledge, maths tables, geometrical information, nature study, geography—the list is endless. It's fun to use, and perhaps this is because it offers a challenge. When the children begin to get the answers right through remembering which contacts work together, then it is time for you to unscrew the box and change the circuits.

Information Box

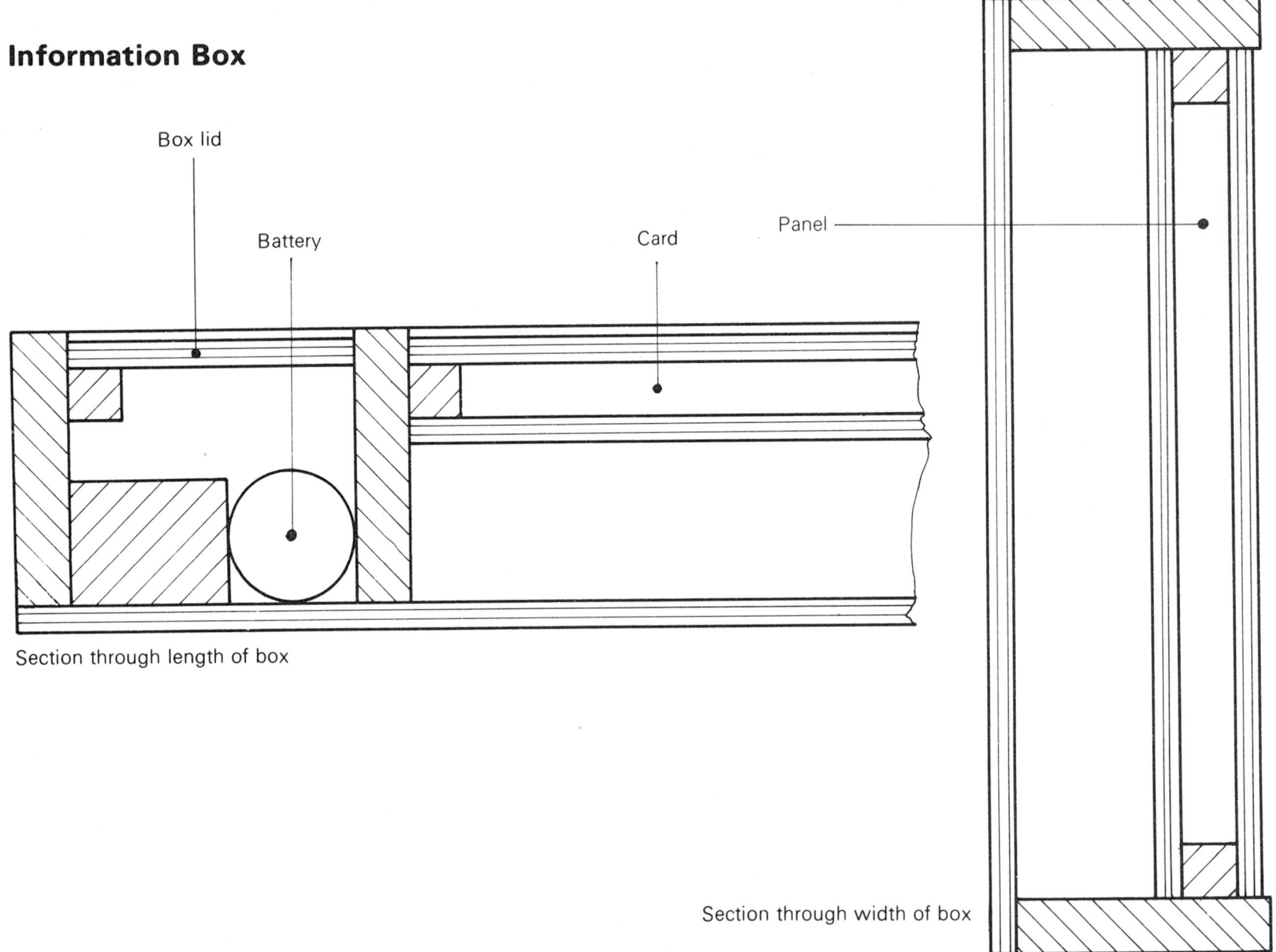

Box lid

Battery

Card

Panel

Section through length of box

Section through width of box

Information Box

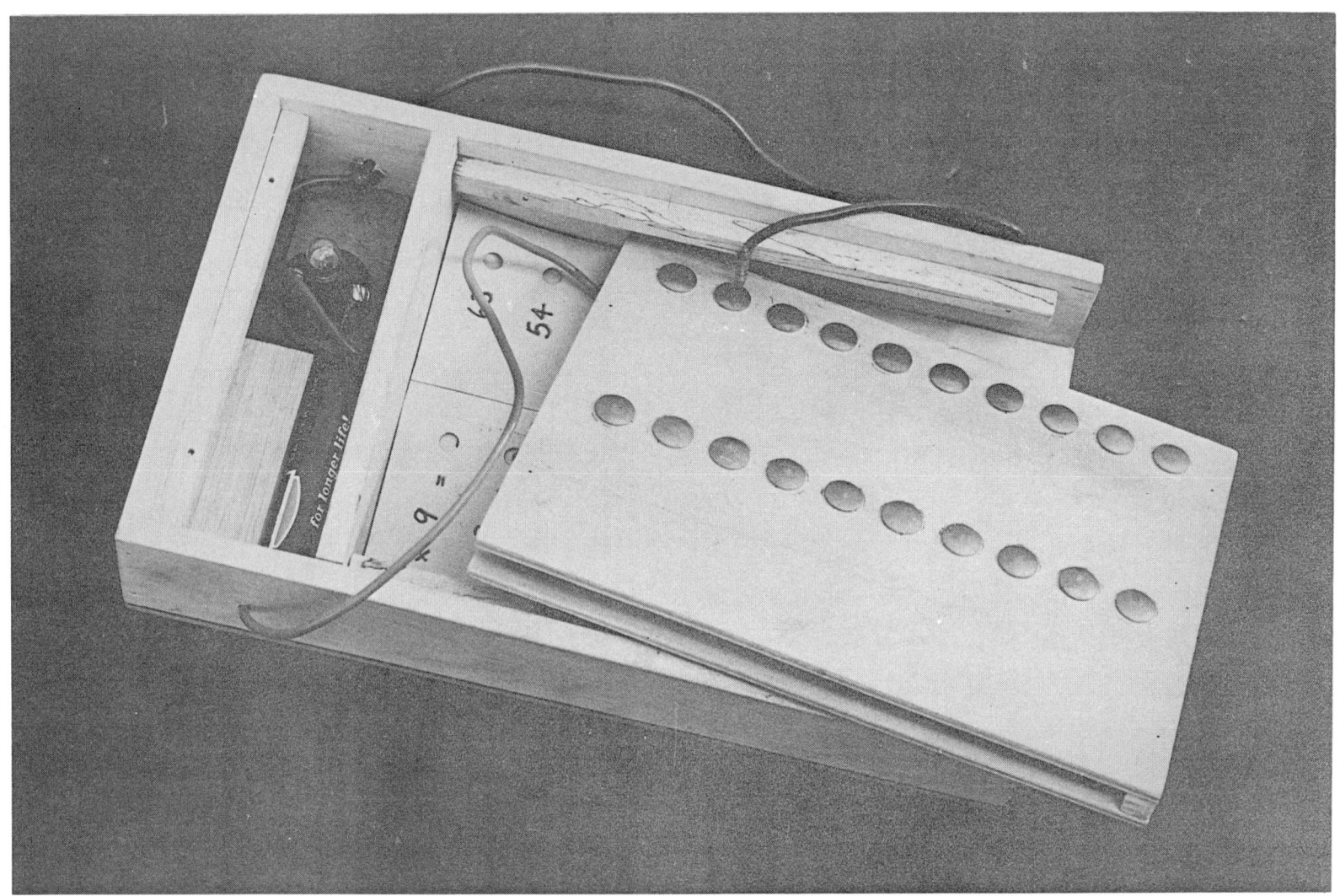

Information Box

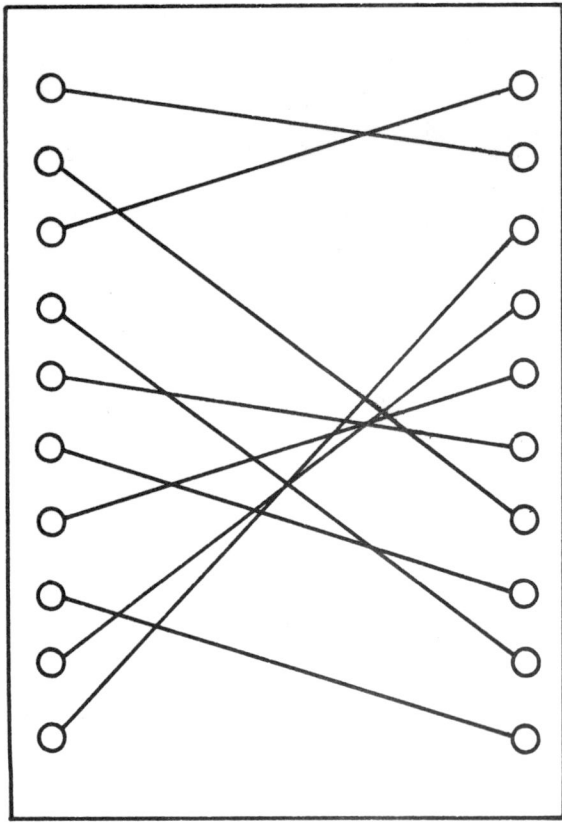

Wiring diagram

O FRANCE	LONDON O
O U.S.A	PARIS O
O ENGLAND	ROME O
O USSR	CAIRO O
O AUSTRALIA	TOKYO O
O CANADA	CANBERRA O
O JAPAN	WASHINGTON O
O HOLLAND	OTTAWA O
O EGYPT	MOSCOW O
O ITALY	AMSTERDAM O

Questions and answers

Capital cities of the world

Information Board

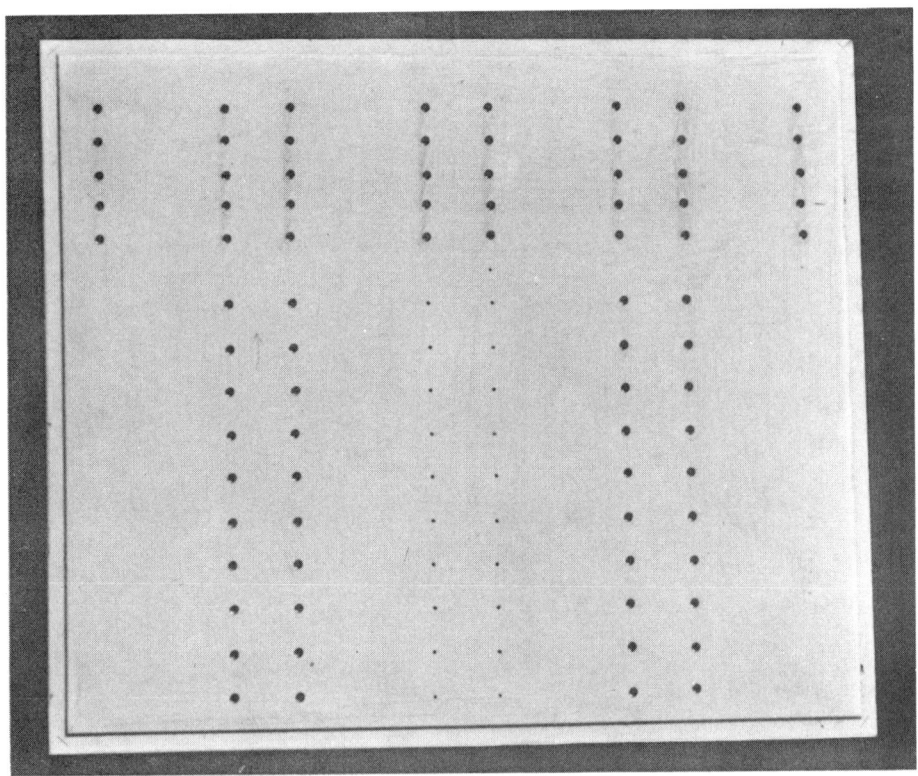

This information board gives room for more questions and subjects than the information box, but the electrical circuits are similar. The questions and answers are printed on standard size cardboard sheet and the $\frac{1}{2}$″ (12mm) holes are punched with a leather punch. A piece of round steel with a suitable size hole drilled in the end can be used. The battery and bulb are boxed separately, or a torch with its own battery and bulb can be wired in for a response light when the correct answer is linked to a question.

Sawing Block

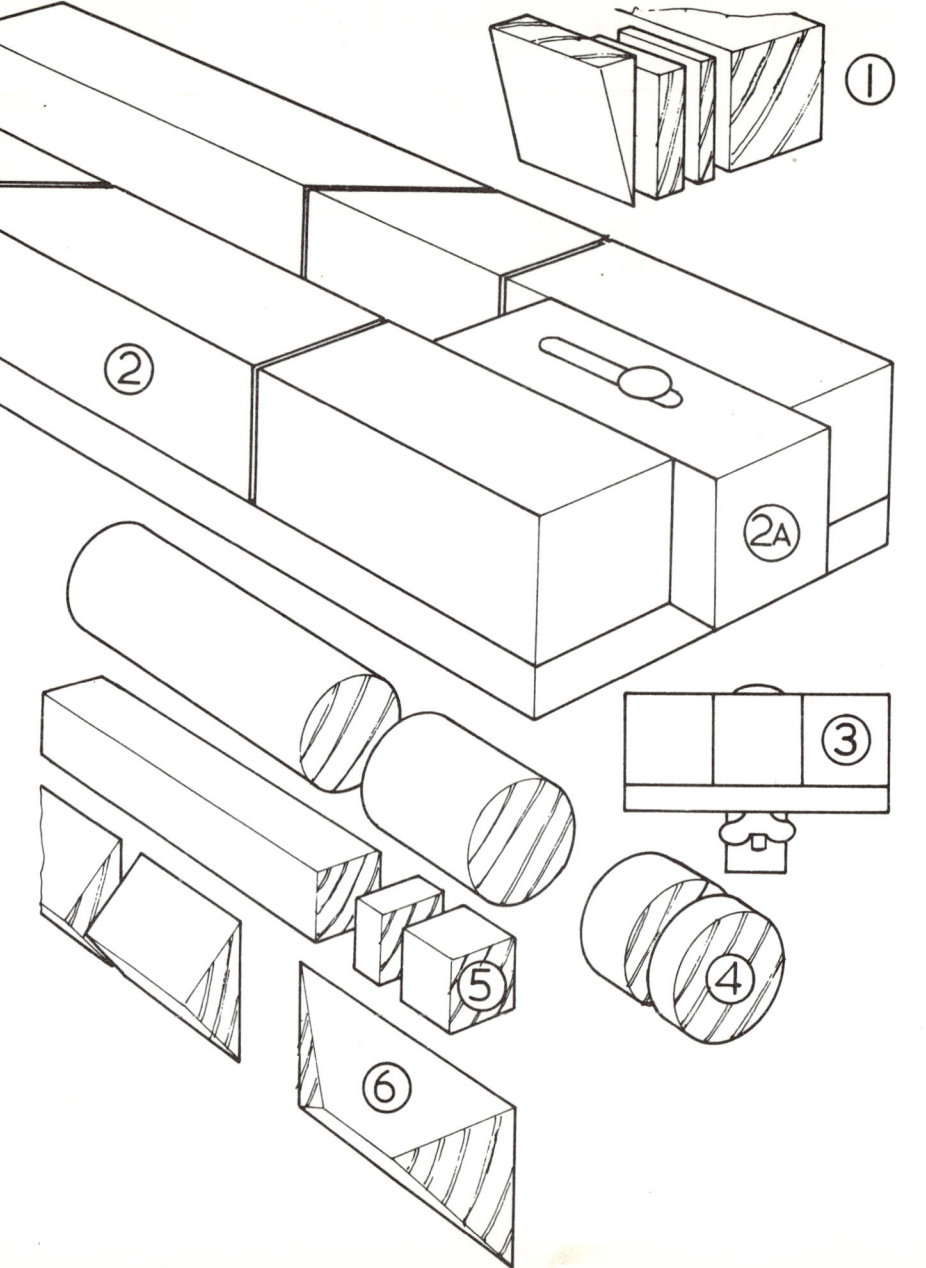

The base measures $10'' \times 4\frac{1}{2}''$ (250×120mm) and is made from 16mm blockboard. Three blocks $1\frac{1}{2}''$ (40mm) square should be cut preferably from beech or other hard wood. One of these can be used as a spacer when the cutting blocks are being glued into position. As soon as the blocks are set with glue (held in place with cramps) the centre spacer block should be slid out and then cut into two pieces—one for the slotted gauge block and the other to be glued to the underside of the base. The cutting block when being used, can now be held in a vice. The 90° and 45° cuts should be made very carefully with the saw that is going to be used for cutting the wheels, etc. The slot in the gauge block should be made long enough so that either a thin wheel or a $1\frac{1}{2}''$ (40mm) cube can be cut. The gauge block can of course be removed for cutting larger pieces. The wedge and spacer blocks are useful for keeping strips steady when cuts are being made.

1	Wedge and spacer blocks.	4	Wheels
2	Sawing block.	5	Blocks.
2A	Gauge block.	6	Roofs.
3	End of sawing block.		

Drilling Jig for Small Wheels

The jig consists of a base board, two jaws (one loose), a fixed block and a wedge. The two jaws can be drilled together and then cut down lengthwise. The drilled hole should be less in diameter than the wheel being drilled. One jaw and the block are glued in such a position that when the wheel and the wedge are inserted a four point grip is established. The jig can be used with a drilling machine or with a hand drill. Frequent clearing of the waste will assist the drilling.

Drilling Jig

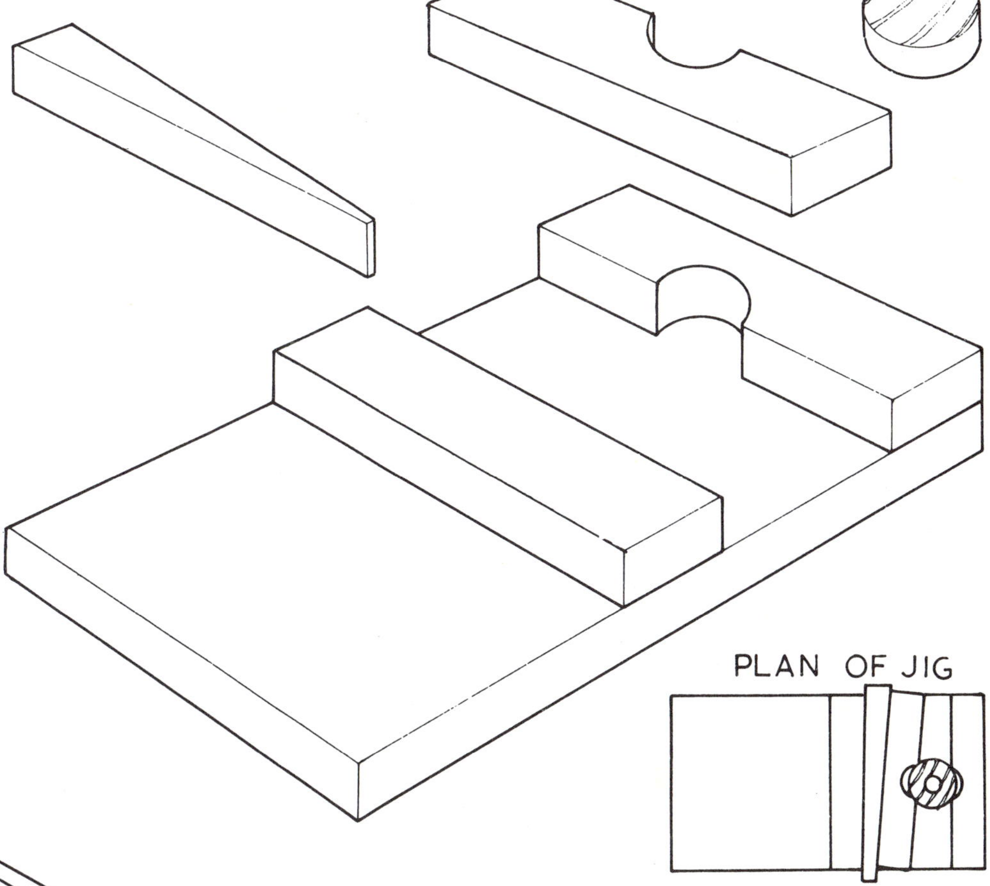

Glasspaper Board

The board is a piece of $\frac{1}{2}$'' (12mm) blockboard or ply with coarse glasspaper or garnet paper glued down at the ends. If the reverse side is treated similarly then this will prevent slipping. The wheels are rubbed around until the saw cuts are removed.

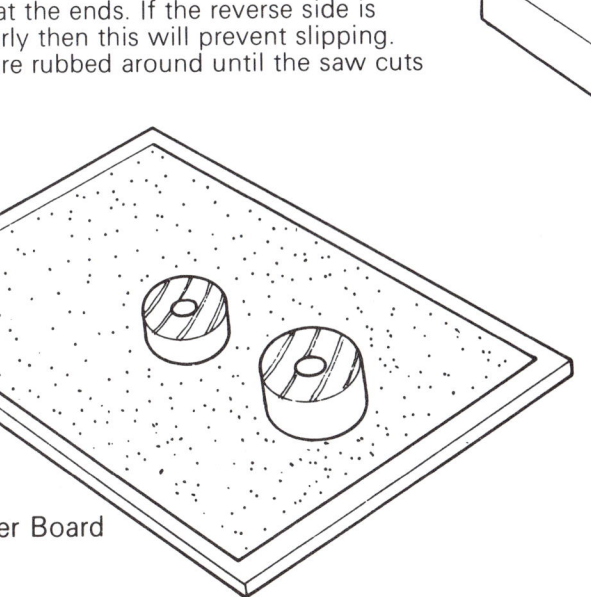

Glasspaper Board

PLAN OF JIG

Paints and Varnish

Dulux Super 3 Gloss Finish Paint (polyurethane) provides a hard and durable finish and the lead content conforms to the amount agreed between the Ministry of Health and the paint industry as safe for surfaces in contact with children.
For a wider choice of attractive colours Dulux Gloss Finish is also suitable with the exception of canary yellow, golden yellow and oxslip, which do not conform to the Ministry of Health's regulations.

Dulux polyurethane Clear Varnish is also safe for surfaces in contact with children.

Humbro Enamel also is non-poisonous and gives an excellent finish.